A PUBLICATION FROM
THE JAMES FORD BELL LIBRARY AT THE
UNIVERSITY OF MINNESOTA

ADMIRAL STEVEN VAN DER HAGHEN'S
VOYAGE TO THE EAST INDIES
1603–1606

Alison D. Anderson

EDITOR AND TRANSLATOR

1997

ASSOCIATES OF THE JAMES FORD BELL LIBRARY • MINNEAPOLIS

PUBLISHED BY THE ASSOCIATES OF THE JAMES FORD BELL LIBRARY
UNIVERSITY OF MINNESOTA, 472 WILSON LIBRARY
309 19TH AVENUE SOUTH
MINNEAPOLIS, MINNESOTA 55455

Preface

While I was working in the rich collection of the James Ford Bell Library in the summer of 1992, a small volume (15.4 x 19.7 cm) was placed in my hands: *The Ninth Sea Voyage* (1612) from the series on overseas voyages begun by the publisher Levinius Hulsius.[1] Slowly turning the pages of this rare book, I became engrossed in a lively and fascinating account of a Dutch expedition to the East Indies in 1603-06 under the command of Admiral Steven van der Haghen. The pamphlet begins with a lengthy exposition on the reasons for the formation of the United Dutch East India Company (VOC) in 1602 whose purpose was not solely to promote trade but also to attack the power, prestige and revenues of their archenemies Spain and Portugal. According to the author, when the Dutch first sailed to Asian waters in the 1590s, they were simply seeking new opportunities for trade. But their success not only in finding rich cargoes but also in establishing peaceful relations with the native peoples aroused the ire of the Portuguese who had been pioneers in the sea routes to

1. The James Ford Bell Library possesses the second edition of *Neundte Schiffart, Das ist: Gründliche Erklärung. . . .* (Frankfurt am Main: Erasmo Kempffern, 1612), first published by Levinius Hulsius' widow and heirs in 1606.

the Far East. Impassioned descriptions of the harsh and cruel treatment which Dutch sailors had experienced in Asia at the hands of Portuguese are given to justify the new, aggressive policies of the Dutch fleets. The following eleven chapters describe the journey which took the fleet of twelve ships around the Cape of Good Hope to India and southeast Asia over a period of two and a half years. This pamphlet provides an entertaining account of the highlights of the voyage interspersed with descriptions of the exotic lands and peoples they encountered.

But *The Ninth Sea Voyage* is more than just a compelling story of adventure and discovery, of European contact with the wider world, for the voyage itself is of undoubted historical significance. This second expedition of the VOC not only marked the beginning of a more militant stance towards the Portuguese power in Asia, but the aggressive policies were also crowned with success. It was evident to the author of this work that the capture of the legendary spice islands — Tidore, Ternate and Amboina — represented a dramatic change in Dutch fortunes. What he could not know was that this voyage also marked a turning point in world trade. The rarity of this pamphlet and the historical significance of the voyage it describes certainly make it worthy of an English translation.

Few works of scholarship are ever done single-handedly, and this project was no exception. I would like to acknowledge the generous help I have received in the preparation of this translation. First and foremost, I wish to thank Professor Carol Urness, Curator of the James Ford Bell Library for suggesting the project; without her assistance, encouragement and friendship this work would not have been completed. The rest of the staff at the James Ford Bell Library deserve mention for their friendliness and support, especially Brian Hanson for his invaluable word-processing skills, Assistant Curator Brad Oftelie for photographing the engravings and Professor Emeritus John Parker for rescuing me from some errors through his careful reading of the translation. A special debt of gratitude belongs also to Mark Vink and Professor James Tracy for sharing their expertise on Dutch maritime history.

Finally I would like to dedicate this book to my mentor and friend, Geoffrey Parker whose knowledge and interests range as wide as any tale of discovery.

A.D.A.

Contents

Illustrations

Note on the Translation

It has been my aim in translating this pamphlet to allow modern readers to enjoy this fascinating account of trade and exploration with as much ease as possible. Thus some of the sentence structures have been altered—reordering phrases, dividing long sentences and interpolating words—to enhance the readability of the text. At the same time, however, I have not wished to compromise either the accuracy of the translation or the flavor of the original. Some of the idiosyncracies of seventeenth century literature—like the delight in using pairs of synonymous terms: "prepared and made ready," "safe and in no danger," "promontory or utmost tip," etc. which may seem somewhat tedious to modern readers—will still be apparent.

Proper names often present a problem for translators, especially in a case such as this where a German work describes a Dutch voyage and is based on Dutch accounts; at times the author has at times tried to render the Dutch names in German. For the most part, I have left the names as they appear in the pamphlet, making no attempt to modernize the spelling—thus "Enchuysen" rather than the modern "Enkhuizen." Unlike the

1

original, however, I have tried to impose a consistency on the spelling: always using Amboyna in the translation even though it occasionally appears as Amboina in the text. The exceptions to this rule are in the case of the names of the ship officers (see p.50, note #12) and with familiar names like the Cape of Good Hope, which appears sometimes in Latin or Portuguese in the text, but are presented in modern English spelling throughout the translation.

Introduction

It was not until the 1590s that the Dutch began to participate in world trade and exploration, but once begun, they quickly rose to a dominant position with trading networks linking all major zones of the globe. This rapid rise to primacy in world trade is at first glance somewhat surprising. Whereas none of the states of northern Europe entered into regular relations with the wider world before 1600, it was the Dutch Republic, the smallest of the major European states in size, population and resources, which captured the lion's share of world trade in the seventeenth century. On the other hand, the groundwork for this rapid commercial expansion had been laid in previous centuries. Since the Middle Ages the Low Countries had been a center for commercial and industrial activities, and by the end of the Middle Ages a degree of urbanization was found in the Netherlands which was unrivaled by any other region of Europe outside Italy. Sophisticated agricultural techniques were pioneered there which increased the productivity and diversity of agriculture, and Flanders and Brabant, in particular, were noted for their textile industries which from the fifteenth century focused increasingly on

3

luxury cloth. By the sixteenth century Antwerp had emerged as the major trading center in northern Europe and a center for distribution of world commodities: sugar and spices from the Portuguese empire, silks and luxury goods from Italy and the Near East, copper and iron from Germany and woollen cloth from England.[1]

Yet it was not the Netherlands as a whole which began to explore new overseas trade routes in the 1590s but only the maritime provinces of the emerging Dutch Republic. Apart from Holland which (along with Flanders and Brabant) had formed one of the three core provinces in terms of taxes and revenues in the Habsburg Netherlands and which dwarfed the other six northern provinces of the new republic in economic development and resources, the northern Netherlands had only been marginally affected by the unparalleled economic growth of the Middle Ages. Indeed the three key economic developments which helped to establish an adequate foundation for the phenomenal economic expansion of the Dutch Republic in the late sixteenth and early seventeenth centuries took place primarily in Holland.

Because of their location, fishing had long been of importance to the maritime provinces of the Netherlands, but it was the development in the first years of the fifteenth century of a

1. James D. Tracy, *Holland Under Habsburg Rule, 1506–1566: The Formation of a Body Politic* (Berkeley: University of California Press, 1990), 10–12 and 21–31; Niels Steensgaard, "The growth and composition of the long-distance trade of England and the Dutch Republic before 1750," in Tracy, ed., *The Rise of Merchant Empires: Long-Distance Trade in the Early Modern World, 1350–1750* (Cambridge: Cambridge University Press, 1990), 103–07; Alan K. Smith, *Creating a World Economy: Merchant Capital, Colonialism, and World Trade, 1400–1825* (Boulder, CO: Westview Press, 1991), 97–103.

new type of fishing vessel—the herring bus—which was the key to the ascendancy of Holland, Zeeland and Friesland in the North Sea fishery. The herring bus was a large ship designed to stay at sea for long periods of time. But the real innovation was the ability to cure fish on board, thus making frequent calls at port unnecessary. The efficiency of this system meant that Dutch herring fishermen were not restricted to coastal waters, and the freshness of Dutch processed herring soon won it an important place in European markets.[2]

Situated in a triangle between France, England and Germany, the Low Countries were in a prime location to engage in trade. For the maritime provinces it was the growth of the Baltic trade which offered most promise. The northern trade was based on bulky items—exchanging salt from southwestern Europe, wines from France and Germany and herring for grains, furs and timber. Once again, it was a series of innovations in ship design as much as geography which gave Holland the advantage in freight shipping. Because speed is less important than low cost in bulk carriage, the shipbuilders concentrated on designing relatively inexpensive ships with maximum cargo space. Furthermore, operating costs were kept low by employing simplified rigging and other labor-saving devices which minimized the size of the crews. These new ships made it possible to transfer bulky goods cheaply and in large quantities, and by the mid-sixteenth century the Hollanders had captured a preponderant share of the Baltic trade and had begun to dominate the carrying trade within Europe. The lack of major merchants in the northern

2. Richard W. Unger, *Dutch Shipbuilding before 1800* (Assen and Amsterdam: Van Gorcum, 1978), 29–30 provides technical details of the herring bus.

provinces also created flexible types of cooperative enterprise which allowed broad-based investment in Dutch shipping.[3]

The expansion of the carrying trade had an impact on other areas of the Dutch economy. As imports of Baltic grains increased—fivefold between 1500 and 1560—farmers were able to turn away from traditional cereal crops to industrial crops, such as hops, flax and wool, and especially to dairy products. Not only was the export of such products as cheese and butter profitable, but this highly specialized agriculture tended to be less labor intensive, allowing more workers to participate in non-agricultural ventures, like commerce and industry.[4]

Despite these favorable economic and technical developments, the late sixteenth century hardly seemed an auspicious time politically for the rise of the Dutch to world-wide dominance in trade. The Low Countries was one of the areas of Europe which had not developed into a united and centralized state in the Middle Ages; it was instead a group of independent provinces each with its own government and traditions. Although there were similarities in the political development of the provinces and although the efforts of the Dukes of Burgundy in the late Middle Ages had created a limited sense of collectivity, the fact that there was no specific name for this region of Europe—the Low Countries is more a physical description than a proper name—reflects its fragmented political nature. In the first half of the sixteenth century, the Habsburg ruler, Charles V, had at-

3. Jonathan I. Israel, *Dutch Primacy in World Trade, 1585–1740* (Oxford: Clarendon Press, 1989), 18–24 and Unger, *Dutch Shipbuilding,* 35–38.

4. For more on the rural developments see the authoritative work of Jan De Vries, *The Dutch Rural Economy in the Golden Age, 1500–1700* (New Haven: Yale University Press, 1974.)

tempted to weld the seventeen provinces into a single political unit, but as yet it was little more than a dynastic union with political, economic, religious and even linguistic tensions threatening to break the state apart. And indeed religious and political discontent with their far-off sovereign, King Philip II of Spain sparked a revolt in 1566.

Never one to give in easily, Philip II responded with harsh and repressive measures, sending a large army to re-establish strong government. Although these measures were temporarily effective, by 1576 all seventeen provinces were in rebellion against Spain. The King made every effort to subdue his rebellious subjects, employing the best army in Europe and the vast resources of his overseas empire. Still, he was not entirely successful: the southern provinces were restored to Spanish control, but the seven northern provinces eluded his grasp and by 1609 had gained widespread recognition as an independent state, the United Provinces of the Netherlands. The turning point for the Dutch Republic came in the 1590s. With the Spanish king temporarily distracted by war with France, the Dutch took the opportunity to enlarge and secure their territory in the Netherlands. By the end of the decade they had emerged as a military power to be reckoned with.

At the same time, the bitter conflict between the Dutch and Spain moved beyond the confines of Europe to the overseas empire — both the Spanish and Portuguese world empires, for Philip II had also become King of Portugal in 1580. Despite the war, trade had continued in the early years between the Low Countries and the Iberian peninsula. In an attempt to weaken Dutch financial power, the Spanish crown imposed a general embargo on Dutch shipping from 1585–89, from 1595–96 and again from 1598–1608. Although the embargoes were not fully enforced, the difficulty in obtaining Iberian salt — a key commodity in the Dutch dominance of the Baltic trade — and Ibero-American products did harm Dutch trade, and Dutch merchants began to search for new markets. In the 1590s, Dutch fleets could be found searching for a northeast passage to Asia, penetrating the Mediterranean trade, ousting the Portuguese from west Africa, and plying the waters to the New World and Asia. By the early seventeenth century, the Dutch had established hegemony over world trade with Amsterdam as an international entrepôt, and until the mid-eighteenth century the Dutch continued to control and dominate both the bulk and rich trades around the globe. It was a phenomenal rise with respect both to its speed and scope; only the English in the nineteenth century ever rivalled the preponderance of the Dutch primacy in world trade.[5]

Foundations for the Dutch entry into world trade had been laid in previous decades, for commercial activity already focused on sea routes and had developed the necessary sophistication for lengthy and hazardous (albeit often lucrative) expeditions. From a technical point of view, the Dutch — particularly the Hollanders — were certainly prepared through their expertise in ship-building and innovative financial arrangements to participate in overseas trade. But until the 1590s the basis for Dutch commercial enterprise was the domination of the bulk trade in northern Europe; the Dutch were not greatly involved in the rich trades which were the mainspring of overseas commerce. In order to penetrate the rich trades worldwide, they needed elite mer-

5. Israel, *Dutch Primacy*, p. 12.

8

chants with large capital resources and international connections as well as political backing. They found both by the 1590s. The successful blockade of the Flemish coast, and the decline of Antwerp as the premier entrepôt in northern Europe severely damaged the economic prosperity of the southern Netherlands, and the emigration of southern merchants to the north provided the infantile Dutch Republic with the needed elite merchants. From the outset, Dutch endeavors overseas found strong political backing; the first expeditions to the East Indies, for example, received not only important exemption from customs but also generous supplies of cannons, gunpowder and munitions from the States of Holland.[6] For the ruling bodies of the Dutch Republic, commercial expansion was clearly seen as a way of weakening Spain.

Above all it was the Iberian control of the rich trade with the East Indies which attracted Dutch interest.[7] The first East India company was formed in Amsterdam in 1594. Even though its first expedition to Asia was mismanaged and the profits were consequently low, the second voyage, led by Jacob van Neck in 1598–99, was a great success with investment returns reaching about 400 percent. Trading companies in other towns sprang up quickly, and by 1601 no less than fourteen fleets with a total of sixty-five ships had set sail from the Dutch Republic for southern Asia, far outstripping Portuguese efforts.[8] However, proliferation

6. Israel, *Dutch Primacy*, p. 67. I have relied heavily on Israel's excellent work for the explanation of the rapid transformation of Dutch trade.

7. It was Portugal which had established a trade empire in the east, not Spain, and it was Portugal which suffered most from Dutch intrusions in the East Indies. Even though the Dutch considered Spain to be the real enemy, once Philip II became King of Portugal in 1580, Portugal also attained the status of enemy.

8. Charles R. Boxer, *The Dutch Seaborne Empire: 1600–1800* (London, 1965; reprint ed., New York: Alfred Knopf, 1970), 24–25. H. Terpstra, *Jacob van Neck: Amster-*

of East India companies in the late 1590s, each one a bitter rival of the others, tended to undermine the profits from the voyages; indeed the competition had become so fierce by 1601 that the merchants convinced the government to set up a single company.

Following months of difficult negotiations, the United East India Company (Verenigde Oost-Indische Compagnie) was founded in January 1602.[9] Its governing body was a committee of seventeen (Heren XVII) with six regional chambers (kamers) established in Amsterdam, Delft, Rotterdam, Hoorn, Enkhuizen and Zeeland (reflecting the sites of the earlier East India companies) for investments. The new company was granted a monopoly on Dutch trade east of the Cape of Good Hope and given vast powers to conclude peace, to make alliances, to wage war and to build fortresses in the name of the Dutch Republic. The stated purpose of the VOC was not solely to promote Dutch trade with Asia but also to attack the power, prestige and revenues of Spain and Portugal. The new company met with extraordinary success: within a few years the heavily armed fleets had established Dutch domination of the spice trade.

The Ninth Sea Voyage, the pamphlet translated here, is intriguing precisely because it describes this turning point in world trade.[10] Here we find a contemporary account justifying the for-

dams Admiraal en Regent (Amsterdam, 1960).

9. The Verenigde Oost-Indische Compagnie is commonly referred by the acronym VOC. For more details on organization see Israel, *Dutch Primacy*, 69–72 and Niels Steensgaard, *Asian Trade Revolution of the Seventeenth Century* (Chicago: Chicago University Press, 1973), 126–133.

10. The full title of this work is: "Neundte Schiffart, Das ist: Gründliche Erklärung, was sich mit den Holl- und Seeländern in Ost Indien Anno 1604 und 1605 unter dem Admiral Steffan von der Hagen zugetragen, und wie endlich in jünst abgeloffenem Aprili mit zwey Schiffen in Hollandt ankommen."

mation of the Dutch United East India Company and its aggressive policies as well as a description of the first conquests in Asia. What was probably not entirely apparent in 1606 was that this particular voyage was a major breakthrough for the Dutch in wresting control of the East Indies trade. With the capture of the three legendary spice islands — Amboina, Tidore and Ternate — the Dutch established a near monopoly on the world's supply of nutmeg, mace and cloves. The ascendancy of the Dutch in worldwide trade had begun.

It is not surprising that in the sixteenth and seventeenth centuries the rapid European exploration of the world should have been an interesting and exciting literary topic. Beginning with the Portuguese and Spaniards, epic poems, chronicles and descriptions of travel and exploration poured off the presses for the entertainment of European readers. As other European states began to participate in voyages of discovery, so descriptions of those voyages soon followed in their wake. By the later sixteenth century, travel literature (though never exceeding the quantity of theological, devotional and polemical literature) flourished in all parts of Europe. The Dutch were no exception. The relatively high literacy rates in the Dutch Republic coupled with the rapid and dynamic expansion of Dutch maritime interests, created a ready market for travel literature at the turn of the seventeenth century. The quality and quantity published in the United Provinces in the seventeenth century soon made them the leading exponents of this literary genre.[11] Unlike the earlier Portuguese and Spanish pamphlets, the Dutch ones often contained lavish il-

11. Boxer, *Dutch Seaborne Empire*, 180–181.

lustrations and maps. Since Dutch was not a widely known language, translations abounded, in Latin, English, German or French.

Even in areas which did not participate directly in the overseas expansion, like Germany, there was great interest in tales of exotic lands and peoples, and capitalizing on such curiosity, accounts of overseas travel also began to appear in those countries. In Germany, two families of publishers—those of Theodore De Bry and Levinius Hulsius—are noted for outstanding contributions to travel literature. National rivalries which figured so large in the age of discovery seem to have continued to the present, for neither De Bry nor Hulsius have attracted as much scholarly interest as, say Jan Huygen van Linschoten or Richard Hakluyt with their respective societies; as far as I have been able to determine, no volume of Hulsius's collection has been translated into English. The works of these German publishers were not mere imitations of Dutch and English ones; rather through skilled selection, editing and translation of eyewitness accounts, De Bry and Hulsius created series on overseas exploration which are valuable in their own right as well as fascinating reading even today for those interested in the European age of discovery.

Theodore De Bry, an engraver and publisher in Frankfurt am Main, began a series on the exploration of North and South America in 1590 (later called the Great Voyages.) By the time of his death in 1598, six volumes had been brought out, and his widow and sons continued his work with a further eight volumes. His sons also initiated a new series—the Small Voyages—on Africa and the East Indies in 1598. (The terms "great" and "small" referred to the size of the volumes not the scope of the voyages.) Both series were published first in German, followed by translations into Latin and, judging by the number of reprints, proved to be immensely popular.

Undoubtedly prompted by the success of the De Bry family, Levinius Hulsius (or Hulse) (ca 1546–1606) began a series on overseas voyages in 1598. Over the next sixty-five years, twenty-six volumes appeared—the series was continued by Hulsius' heirs—recounting voyages to various parts of the world, from the circumnavigation of the globe in the early sixteenth century to seventeenth century expeditions to China and the Indies. The number of editions (69 in all) certainly attests to the popularity of his pamphlets.[12]

The two collections are quite similar: they often tell the tale of the same voyages and, in those cases, appear to have relied on the same sources—primarily English and Dutch publications. Hulsius, however, who had already earned the reputation of a learned man in his native Ghent before becoming a bookseller, is credited with better judgment in his selection of sources, and his accounts are often more detailed.[13] De Bry's series, on the other hand, were adorned with a large number of beautiful engravings, copies of which appear also in Hulsius's pamphlets. Not only were both collections published originally in German and covered similar subject matter, the later volumes were also pub-

12. Biographical information on the De Bry family and Hulsius is taken from *Bibliotheca Americana: A Catalogue of Books relating to North and South America in the library of the late John Carter Brown*, 2nd ed., vol. 1 (Providence, 1875), 316–17 and 467 respectively.

13. George Watson Cole, ed., *A Catalogue of Books relating to the discovery and early history of North and South America forming a part of the library of E. D. Church* (New York: Dodd, Mead & Co., 1907), 2:602; Joseph Sabin, *A Dictionary of Books relating to America* (New York: Sabin & Sons, 1877), 8:526; and P. A. Tiele, *Mémoire Bibliographique sur les Journaux des Navigateurs Néerlandais* (Amsterdam, 1867), 174.

lished in the same city, for in 1603 Hulsius relocated to Frankfurt am Main from Nuremberg where his first six volumes were published. From a business point of view, Hulsius's move was unquestionably prudent. Frankfurt lay on the crossroads of major trading routes and had long been a commercial city. By the second half of the sixteenth century it had also become the foremost center for the book trade in Germany. The biannual book fairs clearly presented an excellent opportunity to circulate new works.[14] Perhaps the most noticeable difference between the two collections was the size of the individual pamphlets. Although it is difficult to judge the relative popularity of the two collections, the small quarto size of Hulsius's publications may have made them somewhat more attractive and convenient than the traditional folio size employed by the De Brys.[15]

Regrettably, few copies of these popular series have withstood the ravages of time, and complete collections of De Bry and Hulsius are quite rare today. The James Ford Bell Library was fortunate to acquire a second edition of Hulsius's *The Ninth Sea Voyage* in 1989.[16] This volume is well deserving of an English translation, for it describes not just any Dutch expedition to

14. Reinhard Wittmann, *Geschichte des deutschen Buchhandels: Ein Überblick* (Munich: C. H. Beck, 1991), 56–60. Hulsius would have encountered a considerable number of Dutch emigres in Frankfurt at the turn of the seventeenth century. The political and religious turmoil in the Netherlands in the second half of the sixteenth century prompted many Dutch workers (and later businessmen) to settle in Frankfurt and other German cities. See Heinz Schilling, *Niederländische Exulanten im 16ten Jahrhundert* (Schriften des Vereins für Reformationsgeschichte, no. 187, 1972), 52–53.

15. Cole, *Church Catalogue*, 2:602, claims that Hulsius's volumes *were* more popular but does not indicate how he came to this conclusion.

16. The second edition was published in 1612 using a different printer (Erasmo Kempffern) instead of the original Wolffgang Richtern. Nonetheless there were only minor changes (like page numbers added to the engravings) from the first edition of 1606.

Asia but the pivotal voyage in the establishment of Dutch control of the spice trade.

The Ninth Sea Voyage, however, does present a few mysteries. It was the first volume published after Hulsius's death, and thus the identity of the editor/translator is uncertain. The dedication in the first edition provides a name — Isaacus Genius — although it is unclear what he contributed to the work.

The question of sources used is an easier puzzle to solve. The Dutch expedition of 1603–06 was the subject for both Hulsius's ninth volume and the appendix to De Bry's eighth. There is great similarity between the two accounts, and at times it is evident that they were relying on the same sources. In both, the voyage is clearly described from the Dutch point of view, and the Dutch sailors and merchants are occasionally referred to in Hulsius as "our men." This identification with the victorious Dutch seamen almost certainly reflects the use of Dutch accounts. Two pamphlets describing this voyage appeared in Dutch in 1606: *Kort ende warachtich verhael* by Jan Jansz. (Rotterdam, 1606) and *Waerachtighe ende ghedenckwaerdighe afbeeldinghe vant veroveren van het Eyland ende Casteel van Amboyna* (Amsterdam [1606]).[17] The later one was almost definitely a source since its engraving of Tidore is found (with minor differences) in both Hulsius's ninth volume and De Bry's eighth volume. *The Ninth Sea Voyage*, however, is more detailed than the De Bry brothers' account, and unlike their version, descriptions of the lands, peoples and customs for the places visited on this voyage are interpolated into the narrative. These chapters are adapted without

17. These are the only two pamphlets listed in John Landwehr, *VOC: A bibliography of publications relating to the Dutch East India Company, 1602–1800* (Utrecht: Hes Publishers, 1991) which predate Hulsius's ninth volume.

exception from Linschoten's *Itinerario* (1596) and make this a fuller, more rounded account.

The Ninth Sea Voyage opens with a brief overview of the beginning of Dutch overseas exploration and the founding of the VOC in 1602. From the outset the Dutch are depicted as the "good guys" who "sought nothing else nor had any other intention at first than to try to establish free trade with the Indians and to do no harm to anyone, nevertheless they were later forced and pressed against their will to change their minds and their wise intentions." The Portuguese are unquestionably considered the "bad guys" who "neglected nothing . . . which might serve to hinder and ruin the Dutch trade in the East Indies." After recounting several instances of Portuguese aggression toward the gentle, peaceful Dutchmen in Asia — the hanging of Dutch merchants in Macao (China), the slaughter of Dutch seamen at Tidore and the brutal treatment of Dutchmen and their Ambonese friends — the author finds the decision to take offensive actions against the Portuguese entirely justified. The instructions of the Heren XVII for this expedition in 1603 follows the same pattern of argument — though much more succinctly — concluding in much the same fashion that "we are forced for the protection of our people and the inhabitants of the islands and our other friends, as also for the advantage and security of the Indian trade to take all offensive [actions] against the Spanish, Portuguese and their adherents."[18] Indeed in November 1602 the States General had commanded all fleets to the East Indies to attempt all possible means of destroying the enemy power in Asia.

18. Reprinted in J. K. J. de Jonge, *De Opkomst van het Nederlandsch Gezag in*

Introduction

It is not surprising that the Dutch wished to see themselves as the innocent party forced to take up arms in response to the cruelty and inhumanity of the Portuguese. The role of heroic defender of peaceful and defenseless people is a popular one to assume and fitted well with the wartime propaganda of the Dutch struggle against Spanish tyranny. Moreover, such a view was easy to adopt given that the Iberian powers had long been accused of cruelty to the indigenous peoples of the New World — the Black legend. The point is not that the events cited in Chapter 1 of the pamphlet did not occur — the Dutch did indeed suffer at the hands of the more powerful Portuguese in the initial contact in the Far East — but rather that the portrait of the good and humane Dutch did not always ring true. The story of Dutch domination of the spice islands later in the seventeenth century is not one of happy natives gladly and willingly accepting Dutch protection. In the Moluccas, Amboina and the Banda Islands the inhabitants came to resent and fear the Dutch as much as they had the Portuguese, for the Dutch were not above strangling native trade, destroying crops and making punitive raids on the islanders in their rigid attempts to enforce a monopoly on the spice trade. In the end, they were little different from the Portuguese in their treatment of indigenous peoples.

But the author of *The Ninth Sea Voyage* could not, of course, know the long term outcome of Dutch involvement in Asia. What he intended to do was tell the story of one specific, mo-

Oost-Indie (1595–1610), 13 vols. (The Hague: Martinus Nijhoff, 1865), 3: 146–147. There is a great similarity between the first chapter of *The Ninth Sea Voyage* and these instructions for van der Haghen, even down to the examples used, making *The Ninth Sea Voyage* appear to be a fleshed out version. It is uncertain whether the author of this pamphlet would have had access to the Heren XVII's instructions.

17

mentous voyage which began with the departure of twelve ships from Texel in December 1603. For this second expedition the VOC chose Steven van der Haghen (1563–1624) as the commander, and in many ways his appointment proved to be an outstanding one. Destined by his family for a commercial career, van der Haghen was sent first at the age of ten to a merchant in Tournai and a year later to an uncle in Ypres to learn about trade. This formal training, however, was not altogether a success: he fled in 1575 after only eight months from the overly strict tutelage of his relative and joined some Antwerp merchants on a journey to Spain. Over the next 23 years he gained extensive experience in European trade, making numerous commercial journeys to Spain and Italy and even spending a few years in Spanish prisons. It was not until 1597 that he ventured beyond European waters, sailing first to the Guinea coast and finally in 1599 to the East Indies as the admiral of a fleet sent by an Amsterdam East India company. This first voyage was quite successful: he made an alliance with the natives of Amboina and built a fortress on the island, though his siege of the Portuguese fortress came to nothing. Returning to the Netherlands in 1602 with a rich cargo, he seemed a good choice to lead another fleet for the newly formed VOC. The voyage of 1603–06 certainly lived up to its expectations, although not everyone was satisfied. Van der Haghen himself was poorly rewarded for his efforts, for he received neither his monthly salary nor the gifts presented by Asian rulers; in 1611 he appealed to the States General for redress. Dissatisfaction with van der Haghen's performance was also rife among the directors of the VOC, spearheaded by two zealous Calvinists who seem to have objected to his lenient treatment of Jesuit missionaries on Amboina. Relations between the admiral and the VOC, however, were patched up, and he returned to Asia in 1613 as the second-in-command to the new Governor-General, Gerard Reynst.[19] Honored by both the States General and the Heren XVII for his loyal service upon his return in 1620, he spent his last years in the Dutch Republic.[20]

The twelve ships for this voyage also appear to have been carefully chosen. The author of this pamphlet makes a point of telling us precisely which of the six regional boards of the VOC provided the money for the outfitting of the fleet — namely the Amsterdam, Enkhuizen, Hoorn and Zeeland chambers. The economic power and success of the Dutch Republic centered on the two maritime provinces of Holland and Zeeland — Holland being by far the wealthiest and most populous of the seven provinces. Not surprisingly, therefore, the initial investment into the newly formed United East India Company (VOC) came overwhelmingly from these two provinces: Holland provided 79.8% (57.2% coming from Amsterdam alone and 12.6% from West Friesland)

19. Van der Haghen's petition to the States General in 1611 is reprinted in *Bijdragen en Mededeelingen van het Historisch Genootschap Utrecht* 6 (1883):265–80. M. A. P. Meilink-Roelofsz, "Steven van der Haghen," in L. M. Akveld, et al., *Vier Eeuwen Varen: Kapiteins, Kapers, Kooplieden en Geleerden* (Bussum, 1973), 43–44, suggests that one of his chief opponents, Cornelis Matelieff the commander of the third VOC expedition to the East Indies, may also have been motivated by personal jealousy at van der Haghen's success. Conflict between van der Haghen and the Heren XVII did not entirely disappear after 1613, for he disagreed with some of their policies, particularly the rigid enforcement of total monopoly of all trade in the spice islands despite the inability of Dutch ships to provide sufficient quantities of food and textiles — previously procured by Asian shipping — for the native population.

20. Biographical information on van der Haghen can be found in *Nieuw Nederlandsch Biografisch Woordenboek* (Leiden, 1911–37), 8:664–666; P. A. Tiele, "Steven van der Haghen's avonturen van 1575 tot 1597," *Bijdragen en Mededeelingen van het Historisch Genootschap Utrecht* 6 (1883): 377–421; and M. A. P. Meilink-Roelofsz, "Steven van der Haghen," in Akveld, 26-49.

19

and Zeeland 20.2%.[21] A later source lists the ships which were fitted out by each chamber, and they certainly reflect the financial contributions of these provinces: six ships (50%) were paid for by the Amsterdam chamber (*United Provinces* — a fitting name for the admiral's ship — *Amsterdam, Gelderland, Court of Holland, Delft* and *Little Dove*[22]), two (17%) by the Zeeland chamber (*Dordrecht* and *Zeeland*) and four (33%) by the West Friesland chambers, Enkhuizen and Hoorn (*Enkhuizen, Hoorn, Westfriesland* and *Medemblik*.)[23]

As was typical of Dutch voyages, the admiral, though commander of the expedition, was closely bound by explicit instructions from the Heren XVII on where to go and what to do and by the advice of a council of war (in this case, consisting of eleven men under the presidency of the admiral.)[24] Indeed the decision to undertake military action lay not with the admiral but the majority of the council. In his journal Steven van der Haghen mentions that on three occasions — at Mozambique, Cannanore and

21. Israel, *Dutch Primacy*, 69–71.

22. Gelderland was also a province and the name of one of the ships. Although there was no regional chamber there, it is possible that significant investments were made through the Amsterdam chamber. *Little Dove* (*Täublein* in German or *Duifke* in Dutch) was the only ship whose name described its size rather than its provenance. Most of these ships had already sailed to Asia; see Appendix.

23. Izaäk Commelin, *Begin ende Voortgangh der Vereenighde Nederlantsche Geoctroyeerde Oost-indische Compagnie: Begrijpende de volghende tvvaelf Voyagien, door de Inwoonderen der selviger Provintien derwaerts gedaen* (1646), 2: 2.

24. "Instructie ende ordonnatie waer nae hem sal hebben te reguleren den Admirael Steuen vander Haghen. . . ." *Bijdragen en Mededeelingen van het Historisch Genootschap Utrecht* 6 (1883): 258, lists the members of the council of war. They were: the Admiral and Vice-admiral Steven van der Haghen and Cornelis Bastiaensz.; chief merchants Frederik de Houtman and Robbert Outerman (on board the ships *Amsterdam* and *Westfriesland*); skippers of the six largest vessels Simon Jansz. Hoen, Hans Rijme-

Colombo — he disagreed with the council and shifted the full responsibility for the proposed actions onto their shoulders.[25]

The instructions for this expedition were quite detailed and overly ambitious, to say the least. The States General — the ruling body of the Dutch Republic — had decreed in 1602 that in light of Portuguese and Spanish cruelties and hostilities, Dutch expeditions to the East Indies must now take offensive actions in order to protect Dutchmen, natives and their friends as well as trade.[26] The political objective of challenging Portuguese control of Asian trade was accepted by the VOC, and van der Haghen was ordered to make a military cruise before pursuing the commercial goals of the voyage.

The Portuguese presence along the southeastern coast of Africa was the first region to receive attention. The Dutch fleet was instructed to sail between the African mainland and Madagascar to the Comoro Islands. From there they were to attempt to intercept and destroy any Portuguese ships found at Mozambique.[27] Ten of the ships — two went around Madagascar to the Island of Mauritius as instructed — spent almost two months at Mozambique, but the carracks from Lisbon did not appear. Four

lant, Arent Claesz. Calckbuys, Jan Jansz. Mol, Jan Cornelisz. Avenhorn and Jacob Claesz. Clundt as well as the captain of the soldiers. The members were nicely balanced between the ships of the different chambers; five were from Amsterdam ships, three from Westfriesland ships and two from Zeeland ships.

25. "Journaal of Steven van der Haghen" *Bijdragen en Mededeelingen van het Historisch Genootschap Utrecht* 6 (1883):294. The diary of the merchant Hendrick Jansz. Craen on the *Gelderland* provides the interesting information that the council of war was called to meet with the admiral by flying a red flag. "Uittreksels uit het dagboek gehouden door Hendrick Jansz. Craen, aan boord van het schip Gelderland" in J. K. J. de Jonge, p. 171.

26. Reprinted in de Jonge, 146–147.

27. "Instructie ende ordonnatie," 259–60.

ships—the smallest—were left behind to intercept the Portuguese fleet sailing to India, but even then, no mention is made of encountering the awaited Portuguese carracks when they rejoined the rest of the fleet in November 1604. Some limited hostilities were undertaken at Mozambique: the Dutch did capture five boats and one small ship (a yacht renamed *Mozambique*) and burned a carrack. They did not, however, attempt to capture the Portuguese fortress despite assurances from the natives that it was poorly defended and that they would assist in fighting the Portuguese. The decision was probably a wise one, for attempts to take Mozambique in 1607 and 1608 resulted in failure.[28]

Following their instructions, the fleet sailed from Africa on August 25, 1604. Although the author of the pamphlet was apparently unaware that the departure date was explicitly laid down by the Heren XVII, he was correct to connect it with navigational problems. The southwest monsoons in the Indian Ocean virtually closed all harbors on the west coast of India from June to early September. By leaving in late August, the Dutch fleet thus arrived about as early as possible in Goa.

The aggressive stance of the Dutch fleet, as decreed by van der Haghen's orders, was turned up a notch as the fleet approached the Portuguese stronghold on the west coast of India. Not only were the ships to sail along the usual Portuguese route in hope of capturing some ships, but van der Haghen was commanded to take a provocative cruise along the Malabar coast from Goa to Ceylon, "making all efforts to destroy, to smash and to set fire to and shoot to the bottom" all Portuguese ships they

28. After failing to capture Mozambique, the Dutch founded their own way-station near the Cape in 1652. Charles R. Boxer, *The Portuguese Seaborne Empire, 1415–1825* (New York: Alfred Knopf, 1969), 111.

encountered.[29] Van der Haghen followed his instructions, though perhaps less aggressively than intended.

On the surface the Portuguese presence in India was formidable. In the second decade of the sixteenth century, the Portuguese had managed to wrest control of the spice trade from Muslim merchants by establishing three strongholds in Ormuz, Goa and Malacca. Thereafter, a number of smaller fortified bases were built throughout the Indies; Goa, however, became the principal base for Portuguese operations in Asia (as Batavia was to be for the Dutch in the seventeenth century.) It was a prosperous city on a island with a sheltered harbor (see Chapter 6 for a full description) which, as the Dutch discovered, was well protected by Portuguese warships.

Despite the impressive fortresses and naval power, the Portuguese hold on the Malabar coast was precarious. By the late sixteenth century, the political situation within India had altered considerably with central and southern India coming under the undisputed control of Muslim rulers who were generally hostile to the Portuguese. The Portuguese became increasingly isolated because they had not seen the advantages of building a network of alliances with native rulers or of establishing a land empire. When the Dutch began to sail to Asia in the last decade of the

29. "Instructie ende ordonnatie," p. 261. In order to minimize the loss of men, he was expressly forbidden to board any ships—the preferred Portuguese style of fighting—but rather to bombard them with guns. Furthermore, captured ships were to be burned not ransomed. A number of Portuguese ships were indeed burned, although a few smaller ships were kept and employed by the Dutch, the yacht *Mozambique* being the most notable. M. A. P. Meilink-Roelofsz, *Asian Trade and European Influence in the Indonesian Archipelago between 1500 and about 1630* (The Hague: Martinus Nijhoff, 1962), 175, contrasts the differences between Dutch and Portuguese methods of naval fighting.

sixteenth century, the Portuguese hold on the Malabar coast was tenacious but vulnerable since it depended on naval power for survival. Whereas none of the Indian rulers were capable of challenging the Portuguese on the seas, the Dutch were. Still it took many decades of warfare before most of the forts on the west Indian coast—though not Goa—fell to Dutch hands in the 1660s.[30]

Van der Haghen clearly was not aware of any weakness in the Portuguese position in India in 1604. The fleet showed the flag before Goa and exchanged shots with the castle, but it appeared too well defended to risk an attack. Sailing along the Malabar coast, the Dutch encountered a large number of Portuguese ships—63 according to *The Ninth Sea Voyage*, 58 according to the chief merchant on the *Gelderland*. Moreover, the only naval skirmishes between Dutch and Portuguese ships mentioned on this voyage took place near Goa and Calicut, and each time the Portuguese frigates clearly outmaneuvered the Dutch ships. Faced with such a conspicuous and formidable Portuguese presence, van der Haghen chose merely to advertise the Dutch presence and observe the Portuguese strongholds. He did hold talks with local rulers and concluded a treaty of friendship with the Samorin of Calicut, an enemy of the Portuguese, before continuing his voyage to southeast Asia.[31]

After the show of force in southwestern India, the fleet was supposed to separate. Two ships were sent to Cambaya (Gujarat)

30. J. H. Parry, *The Establishment of the European Hegemony: 1415–1715*, 3rd ed. (New York: Harpertorchbook, 1966), 80–83; Boxer, *Portuguese Seaborne Empire*, 40–51 and 110–111; and M. A. P. Roelofsz, *De vestiging der Nederlanders ter kuste Malabar* (The Hague: Martinus Nijhoff, 1943), 54–62.

31. Once again, van der Haghen was specifically instructed to hold talks with local rulers. A reprint of the accord signed on November 11, 1604 can be found in de Jonge, 204–205.

to trade (with detailed instructions on the type of wares to buy), and one, *Delft*, after returning the royal envoys to Achin who had been in the Dutch Republic since 1602, was sent to explore trading opportunities on the Coromandel coast (southeastern India). The latter expedition laid the foundation of Dutch inter-Asian trade in cloth which would later become so important. The rest of the fleet, meanwhile, proceeded to Bantam on Java by way of Ceylon and the straits of Malacca.

Not until the ships reached the Indonesian islands did the nature of the expedition change and the ambitious plans of the Heren XVII begin to be fulfilled. A year had passed since the fleet had sailed from Texel, with little gained for either commercial or military purposes. The unexpected capture of the spice islands Amboina and Tidore, however, changed all that. Not only did it crown van der Haghen's voyage with glory, but also by providing a foothold in Asia it proved to be a turning point in the Dutch penetration of the spice trade.[32]

There could hardly be a greater contrast between the way in which these two islands were captured. Amboina was surrendered without a shot being fired, whereas much hard fighting and some luck were involved in the capture of Tidore. The author is aware of differences—at the end of Chapter 9 he argues that Amboina was a great victory in spite of the ease of taking

32. As Carla Rahn Phillips notes ("The growth and composition of trade in the Iberian empires, 1450–1750," in Tracy, *The Rise of Merchant Empires*, 52–54) the Dutch attack on the east Asian bases targeted the weak links in the Portuguese position. From their stronghold on the western coast of India, the Portuguese warships could not effectively protect their bases on Amboina and Tidore. Due to the monsoons it took twenty-three months or more to make the round trip from India to eastern Asia.

it — although he does not (or cannot) explain the background which helps to account for these differences.

When the Portuguese arrived in Amboina in 1512 there was already much antagonism between the different tribes on the island, and the intervention of foreigners merely drove the old rivalries to extremes.[33] By the end of the century Amboina was divided into two continually warring camps with the old tribal enmity hopelessly entangled with religious hostility and foreign competition for control of the island: the Hituese had converted to Islam and allied themselves with the sultan of Ternate against the Portuguese whose allies — the inhabitants of the Leitimor peninsula — had converted to Christianity to attract Portuguese aid against their Hituese enemies. Despite a strong stone fortress on Leitimor, the Portuguese hold on the island had become quite tenuous by the turn of the seventeenth century and might have disappeared altogether had Admiral Andrea Furtado de Mendoza not arrived in 1602 with a large fleet, defeated the Hituese and laid waste to their lands. The Hituese fortunes, though bleak, were not devoid of hope; Dutch fleets had visited Amboina, among them van der Haghen himself who promised in 1600 to come back with more ships to drive the Portuguese from Amboina. By the time he returned, in February 1605, the Portuguese position was threatened once more, and the Portuguese commander, Caspar de Melo, chose to surrender rather than endure a lengthy siege which had little hope of success.

33. Johannes Keuning, "Ambonese, Portuguese and Dutchmen: The History of Ambon to the end of the seventeenth century," in M. A. P. Meilink-Roelofsz et al., *Dutch Authors on Asian History: A Selection of Dutch Historiography on the Verenigde Oostindische Compagnie* (Dordrecht: Foris Publications, 1988), 362–373.

Van der Haghen proved to be a humane leader, even by modern standards: he was not vindictive towards the people of Leitimor, the Portuguese supporters on Amboina; he permitted Portuguese men married to Ambonese women to remain; and allowed the remaining garrison to depart with half of the store of cloves.[34] However, despite the easy beginning, controlling the island proved to be as difficult for the Dutch as it had for the Portuguese. After making an agreement with the Hituese, Frederik de Houtman was left as governor of the island with a hundred crewmen. Within six months the crew mutinied; they claimed that they had been hired as sailors, not soldiers, and van der Haghen had to return in August 1605 to restore order.[35] Moreover, although the Hituese were initially satisfied, even overjoyed, by the Dutch success, the friendly, cooperative relationship between the Dutch and the Ambonese began slowly to deteriorate. Dissatisfaction with the Dutch claim of monopoly over cloves and trade was the major (though not sole) bone of contention, and resistance to Dutch control began in the late 1610s. It was not until the 1650s that the Dutch finally managed to prevail in the struggle. Thus while the capture of Amboina was an important step in the creation of Dutch control over the East Indian spice islands, it was not accomplished simply by the handing

34. Keuning, "Ambonese," 373–74.
35. Since van der Haghen's instructions from the directors of the VOC were kept secret and were not to be opened until the fleet was on the high seas, the exact nature of the expedition was unknown to either the crew or the officers at the outset. The crew was not pleased with the plans for aggressive military action, and more than once van der Haghen had to contend with their insistence that they were sailors not soldiers. For example on February 2, 1605 and August 4, 1605, "Journaal of Steven van der Haghen," 296 and 314.

over of the castle by the Portuguese commander; the conquest of Amboina took much time and effort.

The capture of Tidore was a different story, for here the Portuguese did not relinquish their hold without putting up a strong fight. In fact, had a lucky shot not ignited the Portuguese store of gunpowder, the Dutch might not have prevailed. As in Amboina, the Portuguese control of the Moluccas — the legendary spice islands and center of world clove production — was entangled in long-standing native rivalries. Dualism played a prominent role in the native culture of the Moluccas, in their mythology and language and most obviously in the political rivalry between the islands of Tidore and Ternate. These two islands were considered to be the center of the Moluccan world, and indeed the sultans of each island claimed the title "Lord of Molucca." The rivalry between Tidore and Ternate was difficult for Europeans to comprehend, for while they were sworn enemies and competed with each other for influence over the islands and peoples of the Moluccas, communication and even advice continued to flow between the two islands even in times of war; by tradition Tidore was also the wife-giver for the Ternaten royal family.[36] For the rival islands, the goal of their antagonism was not the total victory and elimination of the other. Rather their continued opposition was based on the belief that the struggle or conflict itself was necessary, and the Tidore-Ternate rivalry was an integral part of their dualistic view of their world. Despite their differing understandings of conflict, the Moluccan and European rivalries became intertwined.

36. The dualism of the Moluccan world is one of the themes in Leonard Y. Andaya, *The World of Maluku: Eastern Indonesia in the Early Modern Period* (Honolulu, University of Hawaii Press, 1993) and is discussed extensively in Chapters 2 and 5.

Introduction

Upon their arrival in the Moluccas in 1512, the Portuguese had at first been warmly welcomed by the sultan of Ternate — in contrast, Tidore welcomed Portugal's main rival in the early sixteenth century, Spain — and they built a fortified base on the island. A history of brutality and cruelty, however, led to the expulsion of the Portuguese in 1575. True to their dualism, the ruler of Tidore then opened his lands to the Portuguese hoping to benefit from increased trade and Portuguese military might at the expense of Ternate. But it was Ternate that profited most. Freed of Portuguese interference, Ternate quickly established an extensive trading network in eastern Indonesia which brought both power and wealth. Nevertheless, this newly found prosperity was continually threatened by the Portuguese-Tidoren alliance. When the Dutch appeared on the scene in the final years of the sixteenth century, Said (1584–1606), the sultan of Ternate, quickly sought friendship with the newcomers; impressed by Dutch firepower, he intended to obtain Dutch assistance in driving the Portuguese from the Moluccas. Finally in 1605 the opportunity presented itself, and thus in this pamphlet we find the King of Ternate (as he is called here) sending his forces to participate in the siege of the Portuguese fortress on Tidore.

The capture of Tidore did not end the struggle between the Dutch and their European enemies for control of the spice islands. In March 1606 a large Spanish fleet — Spain and Portugal were united under one king from 1580 to 1640 — was sent from Manila and captured a fortress on Ternate. Although efforts were made to dislodge them, Spanish forces remained in the Moluccas until voluntarily withdrawn in 1663. For almost sixty years, however, hostilities between the Dutch (with Ternaten allies) and the Spanish (with Tidoren allies) brought suffering and de-

29

struction to the Moluccas on a scale previously unknown. Few areas were spared, and fortified bases sprang up everywhere; by 1611 the Dutch alone had built eleven forts, four of them on Ternate.[37] The capture of Tidore by the Dutch in 1605 certainly opened the way for the Dutch monopoly of the spice trade, but as in Amboina it was not secured until the second half of the seventeenth century.

Another European power makes an appearance in Chapter 7 of *The Ninth Sea Voyage* with the arrival of four English ships at Bantam in January 1605. Although England had been an ally of the Dutch in their struggles against Spain, the relationship between the two states had become more competitive, especially in commerce, by the early years of the seventeenth century. An English East India Company had been formed in 1600 — two years before the Dutch United East India Company (VOC) — but it never received the same level of financial support or state backing as the VOC. The first voyage under Sir James Lancaster (1601–03) had met with some success in the East Indies; nonetheless financial contributions for the second expedition were hard to raise. Henry Middleton was appointed the commander of the fleet of four ships which sailed from England in March 1604 with orders to go to the Banda Islands and the Moluccas for nutmegs, mace and cloves.

From the start, Middleton's voyage was beset by problems: the fleet was becalmed between Cape Verde and the Cape of Good Hope, and by the time it reached the East Indies in late 1604 the crew was suffering severely from scurvy.[38] An English

37. Andaya, *Maluku*, 140–142 and 153–156.
38. Edmund Scott, who had been left at Bantam as a factor by Lancaster in February 1603 recounts that Middleton himself was "verie sickely and weake" and in all the

account of the voyage describes the kind treatment for the ailing crew on the part of van der Haghen who had arrived in Bantam only three days earlier.[39] Two of the four English ships were loaded and sent back to England while Middleton proceeded east in search of cloves and nutmegs with the *Red Dragon* and the *Ascension*. Once more, the English ships ran into difficulties. Not only did illness again weaken the crew on route to Amboina — twenty-six men are named as having died "of the flixe" — but once there, all hope of trade was dashed by the Dutch capture of the Portuguese fortress.[40] Middleton decided that the two ships should separate with the *Ascension* going to the Banda Islands and the *Dragon* to the Moluccas. The conflict between the Dutch and Portuguese at Tidore again hampered Middleton's attempts to buy spices. Although he reached the Moluccas more than three weeks before Vice-Admiral Bastiaensz., he was unable to obtain many cloves before the Dutch defeated the Portuguese. English attempts to purchase cloves thereafter were obstructed by the Dutch, and it is unlikely that Middleton had a full load when he left for Bantam in late June.[41]

The Dutch clearly mistrusted Middleton. Indeed in *The Ninth Sea Voyage* he is portrayed as a rival, even an enemy who is suspected of collaborating with the Portuguese. But in fact,

ships there were no more than fifty healthy men. Edmund Scott, *An Exact Discourse* (London, 1606) reprinted in William Foster, ed., *The Voyage of Sir Henry Middleton to the Moluccas, 1604–1606* (London: Hakluyt Society, 1943), 147. The incident is not mentioned in *The Ninth Sea Voyage*.

39. *The Last East-Indian Voyage containing much varietie of the state of the severall kingdomes where they have traded* (London: Walter Burre, 1606), reprinted in Foster, ed., *The Voyage of Sir Henry Middleton*, p. 16.

40. *The Last East-Indian Voyage*, 17–20.

41. "Middleton, Sir Henry," *Dictionary of National Biography*, 13:351.

Middleton was placed in a difficult situation; he was caught in the midst of the Portuguese and Dutch struggle with insufficient force to take sides although both asked him for support. The Dutch accused him of selling cannon balls and powder to the Portuguese — which Middleton denied, though not conclusively[42] — a charge which would be repeated in later years. The encounter between the Dutch and English in 1605 already prefigured the deep commercial and political rivalry which would become a prominent feature of European involvement in Asia in the seventeenth century.

The Ninth Sea Voyage is not a complete account of the voyage, for all the ships had not returned to Holland when it was published in 1606. The emphasis, not surprisingly, on the dramatic siege of Tidore overshadows the exploits of some of the other ships. At Amboina, the fleet was once more divided, and it was Vice-admiral Bastiaensz. who led the successful expedition to Tidore. Van der Haghen with the *United Provinces* and the *Little Dove* sailed to the Banda Islands where he succeeded in signing a treaty with the local rulers, apparently establishing a Dutch monopoly on the world's supply of nutmegs and mace; the English presented a serious challenge to this monopoly in the next decades.[43] While much less exciting than the victories at Amboina and Tidore, the treaty with the Banda Islands was nonetheless important in asserting control over the Asian spice trade. *The Ninth Sea Voyage* makes no mention of van der Hag-

42. *The Last East-Indian Voyage*, 42–46.
43. The treaty is reprinted in de Jonge, 210–212. Van der Haghen's diary also provides details of the course of the negotiations at Banda. "Journaal van Steven van der Haghen," 298–313.

hen's achievement, probably because it was written before he returned to Texel on July 26, 1606.[44]

By the express orders of the VOC, three of the four yachts were commanded to remain in the East Indies for at least three years in order to explore new markets for trade. As mentioned, the *Delft* discovered profitable opportunities along the Coromandel coast. But it was the *Little Dove* — that brave little ship which had already twice sailed to the East Indies — that truly captured the crown. Sailing south from Bantam in November 1605 to explore New Guinea, she discovered the western coast of Australia.

There are a number of ways of assessing the success of a voyage. From the point of view of the crew and investors, the safe return of the ships (with rich cargoes) and men would certainly be important. Given the dangers inherent in overseas voyages, van der Haghen's expedition was remarkably safe: in spite of the length of the voyage — more than two and a half years elapsed before van der Haghen returned to the Netherlands — no ship was lost, and in spite of military action only nine men were killed and twenty-four wounded. No mention is made in *The Ninth Sea Voyage* of illness taking its toll on the crew, although journals kept by Craen on the *Gelderland* and by van der Haghen himself correct that picture. Van der Haghen mentions his own illness (and surgery) while at Banda and the death of the skipper of the *Hoorn*, Jan Cornelisz. Avenhorn. Craen is more forthcoming about conditions among the crew; at Bantam he notes that six men had died on the *Gelderland* out of a crew of 106 (almost

44. It is not clear when in 1606 the pamphlet was written or printed, possibly after the *Gelderland* returned on April 29, 1606 but before July.

6%) on a journey lasting 12 months and 13 days.[45] Still, compared to Middleton, they were quite fortunate.

The earliest Dutch pamphlet on the expedition summarized the achievement of van der Haghen's voyage in the title by noting that two towns and one castle were captured and six [Portuguese] carracks were burned.[46] From the point of view of the Dutch state and the VOC investors, this second voyage was phenomenally successful. Not only had their archenemy Spain (and Portugal since it had the same king) been critically wounded, but the capture of the spice islands also provided lucrative prospects for trade. But the new horizons glimpsed on this voyage went beyond mere opportunities for trade; they opened the East to Dutch domination.

45. "Uittreksels uit het dagboek gehouden door Hendrick Jansz. Craen," 164–203. On three occasions — November 21, 1604, December 31, 1604 and February 25, 1605 — he relates that many of the crew were sick. It is not clear whether it was scurvy or another illness.

46. "Kort ende warachtich verhael vande heerlicke victorie te weghe gebracht by de twaelf Schepen afghevaren uyt Hollant onder 't ghebriedt vanden Generael ende Admirael der selve Schepen Steven Verhaghen in de Eylanden vande Moluckes, alwaer zy twee Steden ende een Kasteel ingenomen ende ses Kraken verbrandt hebben, wat haer meer bejeghent is." By Jan Jansz. (Rotterdam, 1606). Listed in Landwehr, *VOC: A bibliography*. The two towns are presumably Tidore and Amboina. It appears that only Amboina is counted as a castle since Tidore was blown up. *The Ninth Sea Voyage* describes only the burning of three Portuguese carracks (as well as the capture of four smaller ships and a number of boats). Craen reports in his journal (202–03) that the ships *Zeeland, Enkhuizen* and *Gouda* had attacked, captured and burned six carracks near the Coromandel coast; this episode is not recounted in *The Ninth Sea Voyage*.

Neundte Schiffart/
Das ist:

Gründliche Erklärung/

was sich mit den Holl-vnd Seeländern
in Ost-Indien Anno 1604.vnd 1605.vnter dem Admiral Steffan von der Hagen zugetragen/vnd
wie sie endlich in jünst abgeloffenem Aprili
mit zwey Schiffen in Hollandt
ankommen.

Getruckt zu Franckfurt am Mayn/bey Erasmo Kempffern/
In verlegung Levini Hvlsii seligen Wittiben.

M. DC. XII.

Ninth Sea Voyage

That is:

A Thorough Description

of what happened to the Hollanders
and Zeelanders in the East Indies in the years
1604 and 1605 under the Admiral Steffan von
der Hagen, and how they finally returned to
Holland with two ships this April
recently passed [1606].

Printed at Frankfurt am Main by Erasmo Kempffern
Published by the blessed Levinius Hulsius's widow.
M.DC.XII.

The Translation

DEAR READER,

Because it was felt and indeed has been found, good reader, that you were pleased with the [accounts of the] previous eight sea voyages which Levinius Hulsius (of blessed memory) translated and brought together from the Dutch and other languages, it was decided that you would also be [well] served if these sea voyages were henceforth continued and extended. Thus you will find here the continuation of the sea voyages, namely those which the Dutch[1] took in the next two years—1604 and 1605. Without doubt this one will please you no less than the previous [ones] considering that the Dutch in this [voyage] acted not only defensively—as generally before—but also offensively. In this way they attacked and destroyed some Portuguese ships, both big and small, and some goods wherever they happened to meet them. What is more they drove the Portuguese from some whole

1. The actual terms used are *Holl- und Seeländern* which should be translated "Hollanders and Zeelanders." Holland and Zeeland were two of the seven provinces which formed the Dutch Republic, and so these terms refer specifically to one part of the Republic. For the sake of simplicity and smoother English, however, the term Dutch will be used in this translation.

islands where they had lived and engaged in trade for many years — like Amboyna and Tidore which are the best in the Moluccas — and occupied them with their own people. Truly the Dutch did not originally undertake to act inimically against the Portuguese, but they [the Portuguese] could not bear anyone else to trade more than they did in the East Indies. For this reason, whenever they were able to overtake any Dutchmen they cut them down and preyed on and took their goods. Thus the Dutch were forced to act offensively in order to protect their lives and goods and to save their friends and servants . However, since this subject will be treated more fully later, I will not trouble you here any longer but will refer you to the following Relation and Description. Farewell.

A Thorough Description of what happened to the Dutch under Admiral Steffan von der Hagen in the East Indies in the years 1604 and 1605.

FIRST CHAPTER

The reasons for the Dutch sea voyages to the East Indies and especially why they now planned to deal offensively with the Portuguese.

The great damage which the Dutch suffered some years ago in Spain and Portugal where they had previously — in spite of war — engaged in free trade and commerce is known and evident to all the world. For not only were their ships often arrested and held by royal mandates, as lots of their histories which are read daily by every one show and attest, but their goods also were confiscated without any distinction, their seamen taken into custody, placed in irons on galleys and otherwise tormented, abused and killed in various ways. This was the primary reason why they resolved and finally made up their minds to search for other sea routes and lands where they could engage in trade freely and unhindered and thus be able to hold out against the King of Spain's power and might; for as long as war continued there was little to hope that [the situation] would be any better for them in Spain and the other lands of the King in the future.

In order to effect and accomplish such a plan, the States General in the year of our Lord 1594 sent four ships to seek a northeast passage to Tartary, Cathay, China, the East Indies and also the islands of Japan, the Philippines, the Moluccas and others.[2] This journey and the others which went to the north in 1595 and 1596 were described by the Dutch first in their language and then [translated] by Levinius Hulsius (of blessed memory.) Therefore we will not give news of them here but want to refer the good reader to them.[3]

It was not only these ships which were sent out in 1594 (as mentioned) to seek a way to the East Indies to the north (or midnight) which is certainly 2000 miles shorter than the other way which the Portuguese first discovered and always used.[4] But oth-

2. In another monograph is this series *True Ocean Found: Paludanus's Letters on Dutch Voyages to the Kara Sea, 1595–1596* (Minneapolis: University of Minnesota Press, 1980), James Tracy gives a masterly introduction to the Dutch voyages in search of a north-eastern passage to Asia. He notes (p. 9) that Cathay and China were originally used to designate two different places: Cathay referred to the central Asian lands formerly dominated by the Mongol Khans, whereas China referred to the coastal regions known to Portuguese merchants.

3. The author is referring to Hulsius' *The Third Sea Voyage* published in 1598.

4. Tracy, *True Ocean Found*, pp. 15–16, states that most sixteenth-century European geographers "vastly underestimated the length of the Siberian coast (perhaps logi-

ers have also sought different routes and opportunities; some have sailed to Brazil, some to the West Indies, some to Africa and some to the Cape of Good Hope or *Bonae Spei* in order to go to the East Indies. [To find out] which way is more feasible than the one to the north (or midnight) is the reason that they have continued and pursued [these voyages] from that time — that is 1595 — to the present day to the great sorrow of the Spanish and Portuguese and to the noticeable good of the United Dutch Provinces and the whole of Germany.

Although the Dutch (together with those who are joined and allied with them) sought nothing else nor had any other intention at first than trying to establish free trade with the Indians and doing no harm to anyone, nevertheless they were later forced and pressed against their will to change their minds and their wise intentions. For when the Portuguese perceived and became aware that on their [the Dutch] arrival in the East Indies the Indians were not unfavorably inclined to them because of their honesty and that they [the Dutch] understood how to engage heavily in trade and commerce with them [the Indians], the Portuguese have neglected nothing (in their opinion) which might serve to hinder and ruin the Dutch trade in the East Indies.[5]

cally enough, since there was no reason to suppose that the northern portion of the Asian land mass should extend so much farther east than the China coast whose coordinates had been known by Europeans for some decades.)" However, one Dutch writer opined that estimates of the distance of the northeastern passage were deliberately shortened to encourage exploration. (Tracy, p. 4.)

5. There are many reports of the friendly reception of the Dutch in the East Indies. One such is Jacob van Heemskerck's, an officer with the fleet of Jacob van Neck, description of the first encounter with natives on the island of Amboina in March 1599: "We were closely examined by the inhabitants as to where we came from and to which nation

First they spread terrible slanders by telling the natives of the Indies themselves and by letting it be reported through their men that the Dutch were not honest traders but rather dishonest freebooters and pirates who did not come there to trade but to spy out the land in order to take away and remove the Indian's possessions by force. Secondly, they used plots and schemes in which they, under the guise of good friendship and cooperation, persuaded (and [even] bought with large sums of money) some kings and nobles to agree and undertake to attack, capture and rob the Dutch ships. Thirdly and finally, since they were the masters and found themselves stronger, they employed great brutality and tyranny against the Dutch.

It would be much too long and perhaps annoying to describe all the Portuguese crimes by which they showed their bitter disposition against the Dutch, but some should be repeated here for better comprehension.

Admiral Jacob van Neck, who sailed away from Holland in January 1600, was fortunate to arrive in Macao in the Kingdom of China, as can be seen in the previous Eighth Sea Voyage on page 50.[6] Since Neck intended to buy and sell at that place, he

we belonged; when they understood this, and heard that the Portuguese were our enemies, they were very pleased, and made us welcome; during the two months that we stayed there they showed us much friendship." Quoted in J. Keuning, "Ambonese, Portuguese and Dutchmen: The History of Ambon to the End of the Seventeenth Century," in M. A. P. Meilink-Roelofsz et al., *Dutch Authors on Asian History* (Dordrecht: Foris Publications, 1988), 371–372.

6. Jacob Cornelisz. van Neck (1564–1638) was one of the more famous and successful leaders of the early Dutch voyages to Asia. He was admiral of the second expedition of the Amsterdam *Compagnie van Verre* ("long-distance" company) in 1598, which returned in July 1599 richly laden with spices. He took another fleet to the East Indies in 1600–1603 but remained thereafter in Amsterdam where he held a number of important

RIO.
VCHUAN.
Kidinum   Sichio   Qunsay
NANQVII
Piaenio   Tiechio
Linquou   Liampo
Quiancy
Hilam
CHINÆ
Cambur
Buchco.
Salla.
Chincheo
Ganzao Maio. Liampo
COCHINCHINA
Camco

GAN
GEM.   CAMBO
IA
Ogana
R. de Pu
Uaccla
Petana C. de Polo
Cananiao
Chican
Canboaa
Pulo Candor

Deua
Nagate Meaco
JAPAN
Tons
Fungo
Sierta
Dos Colunas
Una Coluna
Tanaxuma
I do Fogo
I. da Serra
Dos Reis magos
I Femofa
Lequio minor

Terra Alta. Candachina
S. Chaes Luzon
Mandanum
I. Tintiofa
Pulcoas
Sylam
C de Enganno
Moro hermofo
Luconia I.
Ancon Trifte
G de Matalambre
Para callo
INSULAE
C del S Spiritu
Francifco
I del primeiro
PHILIP.
I Uem
Os Matalotes
Sepan
Guana.
Los Ladro.
nes.
Bahan

I de Palmas
I Mindanao.
C Bicay PINÆ.
de Talaon
Gilolo I
Dos Graos
Dagoada
Os papuas

Paror Moluc.
cæ I.
Batochina
Cambina C. de mepin
Crimata
Ceiram
Cailam
I daru
I de Don de Manco.
Aqui in hernou Antoni Alfonfo de melo.
I de Timor
Baixas
IAVA MAIOR

Per Leuin. Hulfium A: 1602.

N: 3.

allowed about twenty men to be put on land for that purpose at different times using two boats; quite unexpectedly they were halted by the Portuguese (even though they had just as little to offer there as the Hollanders.) Seventeen of them were shamefully hanged without any reason being given; the others were sent as prisoners to Goa. They acted in almost the same way in Cauchinchina. For when twenty or twenty-two people who belonged to the Admiral Grustberg's ships landed there to trade (and they were at least as poorly supplied,) they were attacked by the king of that place, incited by a Portuguese monk, who undoubtedly having no companion [Portuguese to assist him] had sought to animate [the King.] Most of them were miserably slain; some commanders, however, were taken prisoner and later had to be ransomed and rescued with two pieces of artillery.

At Tidore, which is one of the Molucca Islands, they showed themselves even more cruel. For when one of Admiral Calthasar [sic] de Cordes' ships came into danger through carelessness, it was given over [to the Portuguese] on the condition that everyone who was on board should retain his life — a condition which the Portuguese firmly agreed to and promised. But when they gained control of the ship, they took everyone without exception, and one after another cut off first their arms and legs in the presence of their fellows, and then when they had built up their courage even cut off their heads.[7]

positions in the municipal and provincial government. For more information, see H. Terpstra, *Jan van Neck, Amsterdams admiraal en regent* (Amsterdam, 1960).

7. Balthasar de Cordes (1577?–1601), nephew of the Delft merchant Simon de Cordes, sailed both to South America and the East Indies. Though only 22 years old, he was named captain of the ship *de Trouw* in 1599 after the death of Juriaen van Bockholt. He and his men were killed by the Portuguese on Tidore in January 1601. (*Nieuw Neder-*

But the Portuguese spirit was not satisfied with these and similar crimes; rather when they saw that the Dutchmen's honesty pleased the inhabitants of many of the East Indian islands who were thus led to despise what was planned and done against them by the Portuguese; and when the [Dutchmen] achieved ever more favor and security, then they [the Portuguese] poured out their anger and rage on the Indians themselves because they were attracted to and favored the Dutch though there was nothing to forbid them. Upon reflection they decided to take over all of the islands and then either to obliterate the Indians entirely or bring them under their yoke and servitude. They would undoubtedly have done this without all honor and put this plan into action had they not been prevented by the Dutch with God's help. To this end, as can be seen in the previous Eighth Sea Voyage, the Portuguese prepared a large fleet of thirty ships, among them eight galleons, twelve fusts, ten galleys, for Goa in the year of our Lord 1601 in order to force and bring under their control all the Indian islands which were not already in their service but which were either allied to the Dutch or attracted to them and traded with them. Under the Admiral Don Andre de Furdado, de Mendoza, they besieged and fired on Bantam. This city, however, was amazingly relieved by commander Wolff Hermans with his five ships; the Portuguese fleet was much damaged, even driven to flight.[8]

landsch Biografisch Woordenboek, 10 vols. [Leiden, 1911–37], 7:323.)

8. Wolphart (or Wolfert) Hermansz. van Bergh, natural son of Herman, Count of Bergh, was admiral of five ships which sailed to the East Indies with the fleet of Jacob van Heemskerck in April 1601. (See footnote #14 below.) Separated from Heemskerck, Hermansz. arrived at the Sunda Straits on December 24, in time to meet the large Portuguese fleet under the command of Andrea Furtado de Mendoza. The battle which took

Although through this unexpected relief of the city of Bantam in Java Major the principal Portuguese attack by water was brought to nothing, they did not for that reason relent in showing cruelty towards the Dutch wherever it was possible. In particular, they did so in the neighborhood of the Island of Amboyna, which lies to the northwest.

According to recent reports, when they arrived there [Amboina] with their fleet, they unexpectedly attacked the island because the Dutch had people and tradesmen there; [the Portuguese] showed themselves so inhumane and cruel that such is hardly ever heard of or read in histories. It was not enough that they strangled and killed all the people they found there without any mercy or grace and also cut down all the fruit trees, but their brutality was so great that they [even] cut open the bodies of pregnant women, removed the unborn children and threw them not on stones but at the heads of their mothers.[9] Such tyranny, I say, the Portuguese did against the poor Indians of Amboyna solely because they traded with the Dutch; I will be silent about their other cruel crimes which are so many that they would fill an entire book if one wanted to report and describe them all.

place in the roadstead of Bantam in the last days of 1601 was the first major naval battle between the Dutch and Portuguese in Asia. In spite of inferior numbers, the heavily armed and highly maneuverable Dutch ships won the day. Hermansz.'s reception on his return to the republic in 1603 was much less than might be expected, for his superiors were displeased (despite the results) that he had attacked the Portuguese against orders. (He instigated a legal suit for slander against them in 1611 but lost.) It was not until 1613 that he was rewarded for his efforts by the High Council. Furtado did sail to Amboina to retaliate for his defeat at Bantam as described below. (*Nieuw Nederlandsch Biografisch Woordenboek*, 5:227–8.)

9. Psalm 137:8–9 "O daughter Babylon, you devastator! Happy shall they be who pay you back what you have done to us! Happy shall they be who take your little ones and dash them against the rock!" (NRSV)

46

Thus the companies of Holland and Zeeland which engage in trade in the East Indies and against which the Portuguese especially inflicted damage through such actions, had good reason to turn quickly against [the Portuguese] with force, and to regard them as declared enemies and to attack them. There was no lack of power or opportunity to put such [a plan] in action. The Bishop of Malacca himself admitted and freely acknowledged in an intercepted letter to the King of Spain that the [Dutch] had not come to this decision to pursue trade and transportation in an armed and offensive manner gladly. For a long time they had not acted in such a manner but had let what occurred to them and theirs at the hands of the Portuguese pass and go by unnoticed in the good hope and expectation that the Portuguese would relent and be moved by the Dutchmen's goodness and gentleness not to act and behave thereafter so violently and inimically towards them and the places which favored them. But what happened? Not only were the Portuguese not moved by the gentleness and compliance of the [trading] companies, but when it appeared that the praiseworthy companies lacked power, opportunity and especially heart to undertake anything against them and to avenge themselves, they [the Portuguese] became even more cruel, tyrannical and inhumane. This [state of affairs] finally provided the said companies with reason—after the high authorities of the United Provinces, the noble, honorable and powerful States General and also his princely excellence, Count Maurice of Nassau as the general Admiral of the Sea gave them orders and mandates—to resort to defense and to prepare themselves to act not only defensively, as before, but also offensively against the Portuguese. In this way they hoped to recoup their losses of people and goods, to secure the East Indian trade which was very important for all of the United Provinces; and finally to stand by their friends and allies, the poor Indians, who were cruelly treated and tyrannized by the Portuguese solely because they had good relations and traded with the Dutch, to help them in their just cause, namely the defense of their homeland and rightful freedom, and truly as far as humanly possible, to protect and assist them. All this could not be achieved unless the great Portuguese power was weakened everywhere, their castles and fortresses, with which they keep the Indians in constraint, destroyed, their ships burned and ruined, and finally all materials taken away which could be used to strengthen them on the sea and to build ships. And in part such did indeed take place on this sea voyage whose description now follows, and as God permits, more will occur in the future.

THE SECOND CHAPTER

Concerning the ships under Admiral Steffan von der Hagen which were fitted out by the [East Indies] companies after they were united.

The good reader can find an explanation of what the companies were, which are so often mentioned in these Sea Voyages, in the first chapter of the previous Eighth Sea Voyage of Levinius Hulsius of blessed memory. You can also find how and in what form the old and new [companies], together with the Zeelanders — that is all the businessmen of the United Provinces who trade in the East Indies — were united and accorded through the mediation of the noble States General and his princely excellence, Count Maurice of Nassau. And indeed such was most necessary, not only for the reasons mentioned in the first chapter, namely that the companies before they were united inflicted notable damage on each other, but also because disunity and animosity between them could have caused great unrest in the United Provinces. In particular, it would not have been possible to withstand their common enemy the Portuguese had they not compounded and held together. And so the old and new companies, together with the Zeelanders and others who had also previously traded in the East Indies, joined together so that they could undertake everything with common power and counsel and would not have to defend themselves alone against the Portuguese but also so that they might attack that power [the Portuguese] and at an appropriate occasion pull it down. Very shortly thereafter, it happened that in the year 1603 after the birth of our savior Jesus Christ twelve ships whose admiral was Steffan von der Hagen, were fitted and sent out, ten by the chambers of Amsterdam, Horen and Enchuysen [Enkhuizen], the other two by the chamber of Zeeland.[10]

The first which was Admiral Steffan von der Hagen's ship was called *The United Provinces*, with Simon Hun as shipmaster and its size 350 *Last*.[11] The Vice-admiral was Cornelius Sebas-

10. For more on Steven van der Haghen and the financial organization of the United East India Company (VOC) see the Introduction.

11. The *Last* could apparently be either a measure of volume or weight. Later in *The Ninth Sea Voyage* (p. 25) the *Last* is equated with 36 *Centner* (= hundred-weight). James Tracy, "Herring Wars: The Habsburg Netherlands and the Struggle for Control of the North Sea, ca. 1520–1560," *Sixteenth Century Journal* 24 (1993):253, notes that "the *last* was a measure of volume equal to about 85 bushels." Charles R. Boxer, *The Dutch Seaborne Empire 1600–1800* (London, 1965; reprint ed., New York: Alfred Knopf, 1970), 305, states that "the Dutch *last*, or ton of shipping space, is usually taken as the equivalent of 120 cubic feet or 2 tons (measurement)," agreeing approximately with

tiansz.[12] whose ship was called *Dordrecht*; the shipmaster was Hans Reimelandt and its size was 500 *Last*. The name of the third was *Amsterdam*; its chief shipmaster was Arnold Clasen Calckbuys and its size 350 *Last*. The fourth ship was called *Westfrießlandt*, whose shipmaster was Jacob Jacobsz. Clunt and its size 250 *Last*. The fifth ship was called *Groß Horen*, the shipmaster Johan Cornelisz., with 350 *Last*. The sixth was called *Gelderland*, its chief shipmaster Jan Jansz. Mol with 250 *Last*. The seventh was the *Seelandt*, the shipmaster Quirin Pieter with 250 *Last*. The eighth had the name *Court of Holland*, its shipmaster Wilhelm Lock and 180 *Last*. The ninth was *Delfft*, its shipmaster Wilhelm Cornelisz. Schultheiß, and 150 *Last*. The tenth was called *Enchuysen*, its shipmaster Claes Theissen Caller, and 150 *Last*. The eleventh was *Medenblick*, its chief shipmaster Dierick Claesz., and 126 *Last*. The twelfth was called *Little Dove*, its shipmaster Johann Wilhelmsz., and 36 *Last*.

Following this list of the ships which were fitted out by the United Companies and sailed to the East Indies in 1602 it should be noted that the ship named *Court of Holland* returned safely to Texel in March of last year [1605]. For after it sailed around the Cape of Good Hope in 1604 it, along with the *Medenblick* (whose shipmaster was Dierick Claesz. as has already been mentioned,) separated from the others with the understanding that one ship would sail to Bantam while the other would sail to the

Tracy. However, he also adds that the *last* could also mean 2 dead-weight tons or 1,976 kg, approximately equal to 3600 Amsterdam pounds as described in *The Ninth Sea Voyage*.

12. The names of the captains (and to a lesser extent the ships) have been Germanized by the author. I have returned them to a more Dutch form: Sebastiansz. instead of Sebastian Sohn, etc. See the Appendix for more on the names of the ships and officers.

Banda Islands; both, however, should replenish on the Island of Mauritius.[13] Because of adverse wind, however, it happened that they were driven to the bay or coast of Antogil [on Madagascar] (concerning Antogil read in the First Sea Voyage, page 16 and look at the diagram) where they found the ship *Alckmaer*, which Admiral Hemskercke had to leave behind in a very bad state, as was described in the previous [Eighth] Sea Voyage in the 16th chapter.[14]

The other sailors who were on that ship were very faint and weak; the cargo which was loaded on the carrack *S. Cathalina*[15] had been brought on land, and the men had been forced to fortify a place so that they were not attacked by wild men and robbed of all the goods which they had. The ship *Alckmaer* had 13,057 bales of [raw] silk and other packets of silk cloth, Lignum aloe,

13. These two ships separated from the fleet according to the instructions of the Heren XVII. They were supposed to look for the ship *Wachter* (whose captain was Gerrit Hendricz. Roobol) and assist him by taking the crew and cargo to their destination, Bantam. ("Instructie ende ordonnatie," reprinted in *Bijdragen en Mededeelingen van het Historisch Genootschap Utrecht* 6 [1883]: 259.)

14. Jacob van Heemsperck (1567–1607) sailed on two voyages (1595 and 1596) with Willem Barents searching for a northeast passage to Asia. In 1598 he sailed with Jacob van Neck to the East Indies and finally in 1601 was appointed admiral of a fleet of eight ships. This expedition (described in Hulsius' *Eighth Sea Voyage*) was a cooperative effort between two Amsterdam East Indies companies with Wolfert Hermansz. as admiral of five other ships. (See footnote #8 above.) These fleets returned with rich cargo in 1604. In 1607 Heemsperck became admiral of the Republic's fleet and was killed in a battle at Gibraltar. Jhr. H. A. van Foreest, "Jacob van Heemsperck (1567–1607)," in L. M. Akveld et. al., eds., *Vier Eeuwen Varen* (Bussum, 1973), 50–66.

15. The Portuguese carrack *S. Catharina* was captured by van Heemsperck on route from Macao to Malacca in February 1603. It was a very large ship filled with costly wares. The silk on board brought a high price on the Amsterdam market and marked the beginning of a profitable involvement in the silk trade. George Masselman, *The Cradle of Colonialism* (New Haven: Yale University Press, 1963), 131.

pewter, radicem China, Camphora &c as well as 600 bales of sugar, 40 *Last* of pepper and 1½ *Last* of cloves.[16] The ship had become old and was no longer seaworthy; therefore they burned it there after they had loaded all of the cargo into the *Court of Holland*; it immediately turned back and has safely arrived in Holland.

The other ship *Medenblick* continued on its voyage to Bantam on the 30th of August.

THE THIRD CHAPTER

Concerning the voyage of the twelve ships and what they encountered on some islands — like S. Tiago and Mozambique where they landed.

As explained, it was intended that these twelve ships should sail to the East Indies, and accordingly, they were made ready and prepared for such a long voyage. The ten which were fitted out by the chambers of Amsterdam, Horen and Enchuysen sailed from Texel on the 18th of December of the same year 1603, and after suffering and enduring great storms and bad weather on the sea they arrived on the tenth day of March 1604 at the island Mayo which is counted as one of the Cape Verde islands, where they met the other two ships sent out by Zeeland.

16. *Itinerario: Voyage ofte Schipvaert van Jan Huygen van Linschoten naer Oost ofte Portugaels Indien 1579–1592*, H. Kern and H. Terpstra, eds., 3 vols. (The Hague: Martinus Nijhoff, 1955–57), provides descriptions of many of these wares. Lignum aloe, also called Calamba, came from trees grown in Malacca, Sumatra, Cambaya and Siam and had medicinal uses. (Vol. 2, Chapter 76, pp. 139–40.) Root of China was reputed to be a cure for the pox. (Chapter 77, pp. 140–44.) Camphora was also used as a medicine, derived from trees grown in the East Indies (especially Borneo) and China. (Chapter 80, pp. 148–49.)

After they rested a while, they all sailed away again on March 14th in order to continue and accomplish, with the assistance of divine help, their intended voyage to the East Indies.

On the 15th of March they came to the island of S. Iago [Sao Tiago] or Jacob's Island. The Admiral sent a sealed letter to the land in which he requested from those in command on the island to provide refreshments or provisions for himself and the other ships with him. But the answer given to him was that they were not able to provide anything except gunpowder and shot.

From there they sailed on April 9th with a good wind and passed the middle line or Equinoctial Circle without any difficulties, arriving on the 30th of the following month of May at the latitude of the Cape of Good Hope; they arrived at that promontory or utmost tip of Africa on the 1st of June. They held a course or route close to the land and on the 27th of the same month arrived at the Island of Mozambique; there they dropped anchor not far from the fortress and rode at anchor.

The admiral called together all the chief seamen and commanders at this place, who after conferring together concluded and found it good that the island and fortress should be reconnoitered by all the sloops or boats.[17] And this plan was soon put into action.

The following day, the 28th of June, the sloops returned and brought with them a boat from a carrack which lay hard by the fortress where it could be protected by the guns of the fortress.

17. This conference was undoubtedly a meeting of the Council of War. Van der Haghen noted later in his diary that this was the first occasion when he and the council disagreed on the course of action. They were, in any case, supposed to anchor at the Comoro Islands, not Mozambique. ("Journaal van Steven van der Haghen" in *Bijdragen en Mededeelingen van het Historisch Genootschap Utrecht* 6 [1883]: 294. The journal is in-

This small ship was loaded with casks which were perhaps the ones which the Dutch later used at the siege of the fortress of Tidore, about which more will follow.

During the capture of this little ship everyone on board sprang into the sea, except for a Mestice (that is, one who was indeed begot by a Portuguese man though not in Portugal but in the Indies or elsewhere)[18] who lay dead on the little ship and a young boy whom they captured and took with them.

This boy informed them that the carrack which lay under the fortress had been there for six months because those in Mozambique daily expected carracks to arrive from Portugal, and then this one was supposed to sail with them to Goa.

When the admiral learned this, he and his whole war council decided that the carrack should be inimically attacked. For this purpose each ship sent its boats well filled with men which soon rowed to the carrack, stormed it and, in spite of the brave bombardment from the fortress, overwhelmed and captured it within a few hours.

Only four of our men were killed during this storming, three who were shot in the leg and the fourth whose heel was shot off.

complete, covering only from November 21, 1604 until August 21, 1605. "Instructie ende ordonnantie," p. 260.)

It was common practice in the sixteenth century for ships on long voyages to tow a boat (or sloop) at the stern. At the turn of the seventeenth century, the Dutch word "sloepe" denoted a small ship or open boat with sails or oars. Van der Haghen's instructions clearly refer to sloops with sails. ("Instructie ende ordonnantie," p. 260.) William A. Baker, *Sloops and Shallops* (Columbia, SC: University of South Carolina Press, 1966), 11 and 48–49.

18. Later the definition specifically indicates that the mother of a Mestice was an Indian woman.

In the captured carrack there were some elephant tusks and Arpuys[?].

On the 30th of the same month [June] two of our ships also took a small ship loaded with elephant tusks and rice. They unloaded it and brought it to the roadstead or approach to Mozambique where it was filled with new ballast and renamed *Mozambique*; thereafter it was used in the service of the fleet.[19]

On the 5th of the following month of August our men captured four more boats [pangayes] in which they found rice and flour which they took into their ships.

On the following day, August 6, they took yet another boat [pangaye] which was loaded with rice and flour like the last four.

Our men made a march on the island of Mozambique on the 8th of the same month with 150 men (who were transported there in nine rowboats), but they accomplished little, only managing to set a house belonging to a Portuguese on fire.

The inhabitants of this island were very frightened of gunpowder, for in general they are very timid. However, they made it apparent that they were favorable to our men since they advised them to take the fortress which the Portuguese had built and maintained there. The stated reason for [giving] this advice was, namely, that there were no more than thirty Portuguese in the [fortress] at that time.

19. This ship is later identified as a *Jachtschiff* or yacht. In the seventeenth century, the yacht was a generic term for a mid-sized vessel with one or two masts and fore-and-aft rigging. At the turn of the century it began to be employed as a scaled-down, heavily armed warship which was ideally suited for patrol work, blockading, privateering and sailing to the East Indies. Richard Unger, *Dutch Shipbuilding before 1800: Ships and Guilds* (Assen and Amsterdam: Van Gorcum, 1978), 50.

They also offered us their assistance in accomplishing this as well as the added information that the Moors who were in the fortress with the Portuguese would easily be favorable to us, since the Portuguese treated them as badly as if they were dogs.

On the 12th of August, our men burned the carrack which was close by the island, and on the 25th of the same month they sailed from there.[20] The ships *Delfft*, *Enchuysen* and *Little Dove* were left to wait for the carracks which were supposed to come from Lisbon and sail [from there] to Goa.[21]

THE FOURTH CHAPTER

About the Island of Mozambique and its surroundings.

Much has been said in the previous third chapter about Mozambique and, though it may not be remembered, it was also discussed in the previous [Eighth] Sea Voyage. Nevertheless, for the good of the reader so that he can more easily understand and be able to talk about reports which the Dutch have made concerning their navigations, we wanted to add something about Mozambique and something on the same subject from the *Itinerarium* of Johan Hughen von Linschoten[22] before continuing with the rest of the report on the Dutch.

20. The Heren XVII gave clear instructions not to ransom captured ships but to burn those which would not be useful for the fleet. "Instructie ende ordonnantie," p. 261.
21. When these ships rejoined the fleet on November 6, it is clear that the yacht *Mozambique* had also been left to wait for the Lisbon ships.
22. Jan Huygen van Linschoten (1563–1614), a native of Enkhuizen, went to Portugal as a youth and remained for a number of years in Portuguese service in India. When he returned to Holland in 1592 he brought with him a wealth of information on naviga-

The Portuguese, as the said Linschoten informs us from the third chapter of his voyage to the East Indies, are in the habit generally when they come around the Cape of Good Hope and reach Terram do Notallo (which lies approximately 150 miles from the Cape or tip)[23], of discussing whether they ought to keep to the left and sail between the Island of Madagascar or S. Laurentius and the continent of Africa or keep to the right and sail around S. Laurentius. Since it is quite dangerous on account of the Bayxos dos India [to sail] between, one mostly sails to Mozambique and from there to Goa.[24] If one keeps to the right [from the Cape], however, and takes the route outward around Madagascar, he cannot reach Goa [directly]; because of the water currents he will arrive too far south and must sail to Cochyn which is 100 miles south of Goa. When ships come late in the year around the Cape of Good Hope, it is not wise to take the route to Mozambique.

The Dutch were undoubtedly persuaded to take the route to Mozambique on this occasion seeing that they had not [come] at the right time to be able to reach Goa since they would have no wind there at all. Those who reach the Cape of Good Hope in

tion to the East Indies as well as on the customs, lands, even flora and fauna of India which he published in two books, *Itinerario* (1596) and *Itinerarium* (1599). Much of the information in this chapter comes from *Itinerario*, vol. 1, Chapters 3 and 4.

23. The name Natal was given because Vasco da Gama discovered it on Christmas Day 1497.

24. The Baxos da India or shoals of India was a treacherous coral reef about six miles in diameter with strong currents located between Madagascar and the African mainland. The original Portuguese name was Baxios de Judia (flats of the Jews), but it was corrupted to Bassas da India. John R. Jenson, ed., *Journal and Letter Book of Nicholas Buckeridge, 1651–1654* (Minneapolis: University of Minnesota Press, 1973), p. 57, footnote #2.

July, however, can easily sail to Mozambique, for they have time enough to take on fresh water and other supplies there and rest for ten or twelve days. Those, however, who reach the Cape of Good Hope later in the year, as in August, must take the route around Madagascar so that they can arrive in Cochyn and not lose time. This way, though, is much more difficult and dangerous since the men can become sick with swollen thighs, scurvy and other troublesome weaknesses.[25]

Concerning Mozambique, it is a small island lying about a half mile from the main land in a bend in such a way that the continent, or main land, on the north side stretches further into the sea than the island; before it are two islands, one called S. George and the other S. Jacob, which lie exactly as far out in the sea as the furthest corner of the main land. Between these two islands, on which no men live, and the main land one can sail to Mozambique without any danger (since it is deep enough there and as soon as one notices that the water is shallower, he can see the land).

The ships stop so close to the island and the fortress that one can throw a stone on the land and even further.

The island is a half mile around in circumference, has a white beach or coast and many Indian palm or nut trees. It also has some bitter orange, lemon, citrus trees and Indian figs.[26] But other corn and fruits, like rice and such, are not found there but

---

25. The most common and dreaded diseases on board ship, according to Boxer, *Dutch Seaborne Empire*, pp. 75–78, were scurvy, typhus, dysentery, colds, pleurisy, pneumonia and retention of urine. It is not clear what disease would cause swollen thighs.

26. Linschoten, *Itinerario*, vol. 2, Chapter 55, contains a description of Indian figs which are clearly bananas.

must be carried and brought there from the Indies, and similarly with linen cloth and other notable wares.

Much livestock and meat is found there — like oxen, sheep, geese, sows and hens — and can be obtained for very little money.

The sheep which are raised there have thick, wide tails which have as much to eat on them as a fourth of the rest. But they are so exceedingly greasy that they are unpalatable.

They also have hens whose feathers, meat and legs are as black as though they were colored with ink and are thought more highly of there than the others.[27]

The pork is so delicious, good and healthy in Mozambique that even though the sick are forbidden to eat chicken and all other meat, yet they are permitted and allowed to eat the pork.

This island has no sweet water so it must be brought from Cabasara, a place on the main land which the Portuguese have named thus.

The Portuguese have a very fine castle there which lies across from the islands of S. George and S. Jacob, just where the ships must come in. It is one of the best in all of the Indies, although it is not so well provided with guns and other armaments; in addition it has no soldiers except for the commander and his men who live there. But in case of need, the forty or fifty Portuguese who live on the island come to the fortress and help to defend it to the best of their abilities.

Besides the forty or fifty Portuguese and Mestices, who are half Portuguese (as those who were begot by Portuguese in the Indies with Indian women are called) there are three or four

27. Kern and Terpstra, eds., *Itinerario*, p. 21, state that Linschoten is misinformed: the meat of these hens is not black but white like other fowl.

hundred houses built from straw on the island of Mozambique which are inhabited by the natives themselves; (they are all black like those of Cape Verde and the Island of S. Thomas.) These are all subject to the Portuguese, and some of them follow the laws of Mohammed like many do who live south of the Red Sea; some have accepted the Christian faith; others, however, are still pagans. They all go around naked, the men covering only their outermost genitals with a cloth; the women, however, clothe themselves from the breasts to half way to the knee with a coarse cotton cloth.

The Portuguese who live in Mozambique engage in trade with those on the continent who live in the nearby villages such as Sena, Macuvva, Soffala, Cuama, etc. which all have different customs, speech and manners.[28]

The [people of these villages] all live separately and fight with each other. Some of them, like those of Macuvva are cannibals. But their finest food is elephant meat which is the reason that so many elephant tusks can be had from them.

These Moors with whom the Portuguese trade are truly faithless like the others in general in Ethiopia, which means that they are not to be believed or trusted. The Portuguese learned this some years ago to their great harm, for when they had traded with them for a time and believed that they were safe and in no danger, the blacks came and attacked them, and not one of them survived.

28. A Portuguese fort was built at Sofala in 1505; Sena was the site of a Portuguese trading post by about 1530. Cuama was the name for the Zambezi River, and the village of Cuama presumably lay somewhere along the river. Macuvva could possibly refer to Makua, the region west of Mozambique.

The Island of Mozambique is ruled and administered by a captain of the governor who is sent every three years by the King of Spain. The governor makes great profit there and enriches himself. There is another fortress called Coffala [Sofala] which lies 120 miles away from Mozambique to the south towards the Cape of Good Hope. Near it there is a gold mine called Monomotapa; in the same region there is also a big lake from which, so it is said, the river Nile originally came, and likewise the large and well known river Cuama or Niger which flows into the sea between Coffala [Sofala] and Mozambique and is full of gold.[29]

Much gold has been found in this mine Monomotapa as well as an unusual type of gold which the Portuguese call *Botongoen on roempe*, that is gold dust. Indeed it is as fine as sand but as good as any other [gold] found in the Orient.[30]

The governor of Mozambique has placed his own people in the fortress of Coffala [Sofala]. When he sends boats (or pangaios in their language) to them two or three times each year, they send gold back to him in the same boats. Such boats are made of light wood and held together with ropes so that no iron nail is used on them.

29. Gold mining had been conducted in the realm of the Monomotapa since the fifth century. This kingdom was situated to the west of present-day Zimbabwe. The large lake apparently refers to Lake Maravi (now called Lake Nyasa.) G. S. P. Freeman-Grenville, *The New Atlas of African History* (New York: Simon and Schuster, 1991), 70–71.

30. Arthur C. Burnell notes (in the footnotes to *The Voyage of John Huyghen van Linschoten*, Hakluyt Society, vols. 70–71 (New York: Burt Franklin, 1885), 1:33) that *Botongoen on roempe* is a mistake which appeared in all translations and editions of Linschoten's work (and is copied here by Hulsius' successors) except for the original Latin version of 1599. It is a Portuguese expression which should read *Botongo ouro po*.

Gold, ambergris, ebony, ivory and many men and women as slaves (since they are the strongest of all people who live in the Orient or [the region of] the setting of the sun) are sent from Mozambique to the Indies.[31]

Only once a year can one sail from there to the Indies, namely in the month of August, as one finds in the Report—to which we will now return—that the Dutch did in this voyage. See the following summary of Mozambique and the figure which is found on page 6 of the Second Voyage, num. 19.

THE FIFTH CHAPTER

How the Dutch completed the voyage to Goa
and what else they met there.

The Dutch, as reported at the end of the third chapter, set the captured carrack on fire and left some of their ships to wait for the other [carracks] which were supposed to come from Lisbon; then the rest set sail to continue their voyage.

As they neared the outermost border of Goa on the 21st of the following month of September they were seen by a ship which came from Mecca, and they quickly went after it. When it was taken, though, they found that it only had moorish and Arabian goods on it—which were being sent to Corepatan—but nothing belonging to the Portuguese. So they let it pass freely and unmolested without any charge.

31. Linschoten, *Itinerario*, Chapter 70, 2:129–30, describes ambergris (gray amber). There was some uncertainty concerning its source: some authors believed it came from whales, but Linschoten supported the theory that it came from a fountain at the bottom of the sea. He notes with certainty that the largest quantities (and best quality) were found on the east African coast near Sofala and Mozambique.

On the 26th of the same month of September they came to the river which runs past Goa and dropped anchor about a mile away from the fortress, thinking that they would be safe there from the enemy. From that place they were able to see the Portuguese galleys which sailed daily in and out of Goa. Nonetheless, when they found that they could do little or nothing to those galleys, they thought it best to move to the north side (or that towards midnight) which was soon done.

In this place they also saw many galleys and frigates and often went after them but were never able to catch one. In truth the [Portuguese ships] were much too fast for them and would row away as soon as they noticed danger.[32]

On the second day of the following month of October, the Dutch ships sailed into the entrance of the river which passes through Goa and put four galleys to flight there.

On October 13th they moved in front of the fortress of Bardes where they found approximately nine frigates which would not permit themselves to come into sight of their ships. The whole land of Bardes, however, was full of armed men which made it seem as though the Dutch had arrived in Portugal instead of the Indies. Towards evening twenty-three galleys arrived there to keep watch and fired four shots against the Dutch so that they were reluctant to come any closer.

32. The Mediterranean frigate was a medium-sized ship of 100 to 400 tons with a narrow build, a simplified sail plan and a row of guns on the lower deck. Although it had only a small carrying capacity, its speed, maneuverability and firepower made it an excellent warship, and the Spanish and Portuguese employed it to harass Dutch shipping. In the seventeenth century, the term did not have a fixed meaning, but by the eighteenth century it was used to denote a medium-sized warship which performed convoying, reconnaissance and overseas protection duties for European, particularly French and English, fleets. Unger, *Dutch Shipbuilding*, p. 43.

On October 14 as the Dutch ships were preparing to sail away eleven frigates unexpectedly arrived there from the sea harbor. The ships therefore went after them but in vain, for whenever the Dutch ships came too close those frigates took down their sails and rowed away against the wind. They did this so well that even the Dutch sloops could do nothing. Therefore the ships turned away again from the frigates and continued their voyage to Calicout [Calicut, present day Kozhikode].

THE SIXTH CHAPTER

*Concerning the city and island of Goa
with its surrounding.*[33]

Goa has been a metropolis or capital of the eastern Indies and lands ever since the Portuguese began trading there. The viceroys or governors of the Kings of Portugal, the archbishops and the highest council and chancery are situated there, and all the kingdoms subject to the King are administered from there. All kinds of wares and oriental goods are found there, and therefore tradesmen from Arabia, Armenia, Persia, Cambaya [Gujarat], Bengala, Pegu [Lower Burma], Sian [Siam], Malacca, Java, Molucca, China and other places come there in order to buy and sell all sorts of things.

The city and island of Goa lie on the 15th degree north (or towards midnight) of the Equinoctial Circle. But reckoned by the route which the Portuguese take from Mozambique between Madagascar and the continent of Africa (as described in Chapter 4 of this Voyage) it is about 400 miles away.

33. This chapter has again been adapted from Linschoten, *Itinerario*, vol. 1, chapter 28.

Die stadt
vnd insul
Goa samt
ein thail Bar
des vnd salset
te

The island is surrounded by a river and is over three miles long, and is shaped almost like a half moon. The entrance to the river towards the city is quite wide; between Goa and the main land there are many small islands all settled and inhabited by the native and indigenous people. On the other side of the island and higher [in altitude] than the city, the river is so narrow, shallow or low that in summer one can easily go through it without removing any clothes except the lower pants. For this reason, the Portuguese built a wall there with many bastions a few years ago so that they would be secure and safe from the attacks by the inhabitants of the main land (which sometimes had taken place.) On the north side lies the land of Bardes whose elevation is just right to dock ships and to unload and load them, which is what the Portuguese have done. This land belongs to the Portuguese. It has many villages, and its inhabitants live from farming. (They are called Canaryns there.) These Canaryns are mostly Christian, but in dress they follow the customs of the natives, so that they cover nothing on their whole bodies except the genitals.

An extremely large number of Indian palm trees whose nut is called a coconut (and these are now quite familiar) are found on this island of Bardes. The river which separates Bardes from the main land is so small that it can hardly be seen and discerned between Bardes and the main land when one is somewhat far away.

Towards the south of the Island of Goa where the river flows again into the sea, there is an island called Salsette which is very like and similar to Bardes. Besides the many other tiny islands which lie between Goa and Salsette and which are all full of palm trees, there is another island near the mouth of the river which is called Goa Velha, that is old Goa; nothing of any value grows on it.

Both the Islands of Salsette and Bardes are let out by the King of Portugal, and from these rents and incomes the viceroys and the other royal servants are paid; maintenance for the archbishops and other men of clerical standing is also provided from these rents and incomes.

Concerning the island itself, it is full of mountains and at many places so desert-like that it is hardly possible, without great effort and work, to go from the city over the land to the entrance of the river and the sea coast. There are, however, many villages; as already mentioned, most of them are built around the edge by the sea and the river, but there are also some next to tiny inland lakes which are inhabited by the Canaryns. And that is the reason why there are so many Indian palm trees or coconut trees in the villages and by the canaryn houses, namely that these [trees] like to grow not on mountains but only in low, wet and marshy places.

The river which flows from the sea to Goa has some curved places and is so deep that ships of 100 *Last* (which is approximately 3600 hundred-weight) can sail on it up to the city and are even able to unload there.

The Portuguese carracks, however, must be unloaded on Bardes because of their weight, but once that is done, they can sail to the city of Goa if they want.

The city of Goa is well built in the style and manner of the houses and streets in Lisbon and elsewhere in Portugal. The houses, however, are in general somewhat lower on account of the great heat, and most of them have courtyards, trees and gardens in which all sorts of delightful and sweet Indian plants are found. There are also many cloisters, colleges and churches in the city, as in Lisbon, with the exception of female cloisters; women are not brought there [Goa] so that they can close themselves away, and they should not be allowed to separate themselves from the company of men who often respect them more than their own lives.

The island remains green in both summer and winter. Indeed when some of the trees have born their fruit and become faded, there are always others which are just beginning to flower and turn green; it really is delightful to behold.

As in Lisbon, the city contains some hills and valleys. It was at one time quite small and encircled by a wall and ditch; the wall still stands today but the gates have all been broken out and the city has expanded so much that the part outside the wall is twice as big as the part inside. This newly added part of the city is without walls and fortifications. Only the eastern side of the island has a wall which stretches across from the island of Salsette.

The whole island has no fortress except on the heights of Bardes at the entrance of the river where there is an old fortress provided with two or three iron guns and a wall on which a watch is held at night. The defense and preservation of Goa consists of three or four gates built on the eastern side, hard by the river across from the main land and [Islands of] Salsette and Bardes. Each one has a captain and clerk who keep watch so that no one may come over to the island unless he is let and permitted by the captain.

When the Indian Decanyns (those are the ones who are born in the land Decam which is commonly called Ballagate and lies behind Goa; many have their homes and wares in Goa) and other Moors and heathens want to go across to the main land, in order to buy personal supplies and other wares, they must have a mark pressed on their bare arms at the gates (which are called Passos) and they must show [the mark] on their return. To obtain this mark they must pay two basaruken, which is approximately a half heller, and the money goes to the captain and clerk. At night they have a boy who rings a small bell on the gate, and that is all the watch that is kept on the island. There are five such gates: the first is called *Passo de S. Iago*, since the parish[34] is St. James's. The second is called *o passo seco*, that is dry crossing, seeing that the river is there at its narrowest and shallowest. The third gate on the south side of the island does not lie far from the city and is called *o passo de Daugyn* or Mother of God. The wall — as already mentioned — stretches from the *passo di Bensteryn* or S. Iago to the next gate or crossing. The rest of the island is bare and without any type of protection.

The fourth gate is the *o passo de Norvva*. The fifth and last lies half way along the river's southern side towards Bardes and is the strongest of the gates and the best armed. It is called *o passo de Pangyn*. Here one can go over to Bardes and all ships and boats which want to go in or out must go past it where they are inspected by those on watch.

Concerning the government at Goa, it is done much the same way as in Portugal. They live there next to the Indians: heathens, Moors, Jews, Armenians, Gujarats, Banians, Brumenes and all sorts of Indian peoples who all live according to their own beliefs and laws without being forced by anyone to do anything contrary to them.

34. The word used is "Kaspel." It is not clear if it meant "Kapelle" = chapel. Linschoten, *Itinerario*, p. 135 uses the word "parochie" clearly meaning the parish of St. James.

The only thing which they are forbidden to do is to burn their dead in the city and on the island and openly to practice their superstitious and devilish customs. Outside of the island and in their own homes they are permitted to perform their ceremonies.

All the inhabitants of the island without exception are subject to [Portuguese] ordinances which are put into effect by the Portuguese in their own manner. However, if someone has been baptized and becomes a Christian and then profanes and dirties himself with heathen superstitions, he falls into the hands of the [Catholic] Inquisition and can in no way be freed from their censure and punishment.

Because the Island of Goa has many hills and is very desolate, it has little livestock on it; thus beasts, namely chickens, sows, eggs and milk and the like have to be brought from Salsette, Bardes and especially the main land. Corn, rice and other grains, likewise oil and similar [commodities], are brought there from Cambaya and the borders of Malabar. They have so much excess palm wine that they can supply others with it but no sweet water except for a well called Bangauyn which is almost half an hour away from the city and supplies the entire city. This water is very good to drink and is brought for sale by servants in jugs and carried all around the city.

The whole land is dry and full of stones and dry, and the earth is somewhat red; so that some Italian alchemists reckon that they could melt copper and gold out of it. But up until now the King and governor have not wanted to allow and permit this because they feared that if such [metals] were found, the place would be attacked by the surrounding enemies. See the following diagram of the city and Island of Goa which should help you to a better grasp and understanding of that which has just been explained in this chapter.

The Seventh Chapter

How the Dutch traveled from Goa to Calicout, what happened to them in Cananor and how they came to and concluded a perpetual alliance with the King of Calicout as well as all that happened to them until January 17, 1605.

They arrived before the city of Cananor [Cannanore] on the 26th of October and cast out their anchor very near to the fortress of the said city. The admiral immediately sent a boat with a peace flag to land so that he could converse with the inhabitants. But when the boat arrived on land the Portuguese who lay hidden behind the rocks shot at it; the Dutch immediately returned fire. The Moors looked on and did not assist either party in the least.

In the afternoon some of the Moors came with a peace flag to the admiral on behalf of their king bringing him a letter from the king with the [following] content: He, the king, had already heard much about the Dutch, in particular that they were the declared enemies of the Portuguese. He supposed that the Dutch intended to attack and damage the [Portuguese] fortress since they had taken position under it; he would not advise them to do so at this time seeing that it was very strong and well supplied with all necessities. Moreover, for 102 years he and his ancestors had been protected and ruled by the Portuguese, and he intended to continue [with this arrangement] hereafter. Therefore he advised them to depart and (if they wanted to be his friend) not to attack or do any damage to the fortress or to any of his Maldive islands or his ships. In return he wanted to show himself a friend to them. Since the case was put so firmly to them, the Dutch sailed away and set out for Calicout.

On October 27th they arrived at the entrance to Calicout and dispatched the vice-admiral as their envoy along with the chief merchant Holtzmann[35] and some others to strike an alliance with the King of Calicout and his [subjects.]

But when these envoys were ready and wanted to make for land in their boat, nine frigates appeared and held their course as close to the land as possible.

The Dutch pursued them immediately with their sloops but did not scare the frigates in the least; indeed they went right towards them without any timidity. When the Dutch observed this and that the frigates would slip away from the sloops, they sent skiffs or larger boats to assist, and they managed to block the path of the frigates. They overtook one of the frigates, but when they attacked and boarded it, all the people who were on it jumped into the sea. There were 80 men on board, all Moors ex-

35. Frederik de Houtman (1540–1627) was already an experienced seaman having gone on both of the ill-fated voyages of his elder brother Cornelis de Houtman when he was chosen to sail with van der Haghen as chief merchant of the *Amsterdam*. It was intended that he should remain in the Indies as a factor at Patane, but as will be seen below, he was instead appointed governor of Amboina after its capture in 1605. ("Extract uit eene Memorie voor den Admirael Steven Verhagen . . ." in J. K. J. de Jonge, *De Opkomst van het Nederlandsch Gezag in Ooost-Indie [1595–1610]*, 13 vols. [The Hague: Martinus Nijhoff, 1862–88], 3:147–8.) Later, in 1616, he was named to the Raad van Indie and made governor of the Moluccas. He was a skilled governor as well as a talented linguist; in 1603 he published a dictionary of Malaysian and Madagascan languages compiled during two years of imprisonment at Achin. Returning from Asia in 1625 he settled in Alkmaar for the last years of his life. (*Nieuw Nederlandsch Biografisch Woordenboek*, 7:627; and Masselman, pp. 88–96 and 120–23.)

cept for 15 Portuguese. Six of them were killed, six taken captive and three died in swimming. In this little ship there were 25 one-ton boxes of gunpowder which they had intended to take to their fortress on the island of Ceylon.

In the night of October 31st, about the eleventh hour they left Calicout in order to pick up the vice-admiral who had accompanied the sloops from the Dutch ships to the land and had remained there until the morning of the second day.

On November 30th [sic 3rd?] four envoys on behalf of the king came to the admiral's ship and announced that they wanted to show them where the king with his entire army lay encamped. So the ships immediately weighed anchor and sailed to the indicated place.

Now as they went they became aware on the next day of nineteen Portuguese frigates not far from the shore.

The ship *Gelderland* which saw them before all the others seized the advantage and greeted them courageously with its guns. In all 63 shots were fired from the great guns on the frigates by the *Gelderland* and the other ships. As a result the frigates suffered much damage and were completely disarmed. Nevertheless, they did not capture any of them because the weather became suddenly very still making it impossible to maneuver the ships. The frigates seemed to be quite safe from the sloops since they appeared to be well provided with people and all kinds of munitions and other necessaries. Only later was it learned from the inhabitants that their crews had suffered great damage.

The frigates were not yet out of the sight when the Dutch saw two junks laying [nearby.] They immediately leapt upon them and captured them since the four Calicout envoys reported that they belonged to the Portuguese. Many coconuts were found in them.

On the sixth of the same month [November] the three ships which had been left behind to wait for the carracks from Lisbon, namely *Enchuysen, Delfft, Little Dove* and the yacht *Mozam-bique*, came safely to the other ships and thus the whole fleet arrived on the same day not far from the place where the king had set up his camp; there they also dropped their anchors and rode at anchor.

On November 8th the Samoryn himself—that is the Emperor from Malabar, the King of Calicout[36]—wanted to talk with the admiral in order to negotiate and conclude a perpetual peace. He had decided on this [step] mainly because he perceived that the Dutch were the declared enemies of the Portuguese. Indeed such [information] had come to him before through common gossip, but now he observed it daily through their deeds. Thus he had no doubt that the Dutch would be good and true friends to him.

When the ships learned this through their appointed envoys, they unanimously decided that the admiral should go in person on land along with the merchants, Holtzmann, Compostel and Ontermann as well as the shipmaster Nickels Thyssen[37] and some others who were appointed because of their position. This

36. Samorin, from a Sanskrit word meaning sea king, was a title used by the most powerful princes on the Malabar coast.

37. De Jonge, 3:27–28, names de Houtman as chief merchant on board the *Amsterdam*, Hendrick Jacobsz. Compostel as chief merchant on the *Hoorn* and Robbert Outerman as chief merchant on the *Westfriesland*. The shipmaster of the *Enchuysen* is listed above as Claes Theissen. This could be the same name as Nickels Thyssen. Hendrick Jansz. Craen, chief merchant on the *Gelderland* says in his diary that he was also among those who accompanied the admiral; he provides an eyewitness account of the meeting

was all done with a stately splendor. As they greeted the king upon their arrival, they made some reverences which he accepted genially and gratefully. Afterwards he concluded a perpetual peace with them which was confirmed with an oath, openly and with all solemnities and gracefulness on both sides.

A letter was also composed about [the peace] which the king earnestly desired to be sent to Holland and Zeeland for further assurance that his lands would remain open at all times for free trade and pursuit of business.

In general the people of Malabar were very pleased about such an alliance.

After concluding the alliance, the admiral took his leave from the king with all respect and returned cheerfully with all of his men to the ships.

Now since all the ships were together again, it was thought advisable to begin to think about trade. Therefore the ships *Seelandt* and *Enchuysen* were sent to Cambaya [Gujarat] to engage in the business of buying and selling. The rest, though, went to see Cochyn, for while making the alliance with the King of Calicout, the admiral had—upon his request—firmly agreed and promised that he would do so.

On November 14th as the sun was setting the admiral arrived in Cochyn with the remaining ships and they went so close to the city that they could see the ships which lay in the harbor. It was a beautiful city to look at. But since it would have been dangerous to sail into a harbor whose features were unfamiliar to them, they changed their course and sailed to Ceylon arriving

with the Samorin. ("Uittreksels uit het dagboek gehouden door Hendrick Jansz. Craen" in de Jonge, 3:172–75.)

there on the 22nd and anchoring by the city of Colombo. They fired some shots at the fortress which did not neglect to greet each ship with a shot in answer; therefore the ships sailed away from there.[38]

On December 13th they came to the island of Sumatra, formerly called Tabrobuna and Aurea Chersonesus, and there the ship *Delfft* separated from the others in order to take the envoys of the King of Achyn back to Achyn.[39]

On the 31st of the said month [December] they reached Bantam where they learned that one of their ships, namely the *Court of Holland* (which, as mentioned before, was separated from the fleet) had taken on the cargo of the ship *Alckmaer*, which had remained in Antogil Bay on the island of Madagascar

38. The best variety of cinnamon was grown on the lowlands of Ceylon which came under Portuguese control in the sixteenth century. Since only inferior sorts were grown elsewhere—as on the Malabar coast—the Portuguese held an effective monopoly on cinnamon until challenged by the Dutch at the turn of the seventeenth century. A disastrous attempt was made in June 1603 under Sebald de Weert to oust the Portuguese from Ceylon with local assistance resulting in the slaughter of Dutch seamen. A much more determined effort began in 1638, but it took twenty years before control of Ceylon passed to Dutch hands. The city of Colombo itself was captured in 1656. Van der Haghen's instructions foresaw a five or six day stay at Ceylon for trade only, and he apparently disagreed with the council's plan to fire on the fortress. ("Instructie ende ordonnantie," p. 262 and "Journaal van Steven van der Haghen," p. 294.)

39. Cornelis Bastiaensz. had brought the Achin envoys to the Dutch Republic in 1602 on a ship outfitted by the United Zeeland Company. (M. Antoinette P. Roelofsz, *De Vestiging der Nederlanders ter Kuste Malabar*, Verhandelingen van het Koninklijk Instituut voor de Taal-, Land-, en Volkenkunde van Nederlandsch-Indie, deel 4 [The Hague: Martinus Nijhoff, 1943], 33.) Achin lies on the northwest tip of the island of Sumatra, and by the second half of the sixteenth century it had become the most important Sumatran kingdom. It exported several valuable commodities to China, India and Malacca, namely pepper, benzoin and gold. (Charles R. Boxer, *The Portuguese Seaborne Empire 1415–1825* [New York: Alfred Knopf, 1969], 42–43.) The author has once again copied an error from Linschoten: Taprobana was the name for Ceylon not Sumatra.

or S. Laurentius; thus it could not go on and planned to travel back to Holland.[40]

They also found that the house of those who always remained [in Bantam] to buy and sell wares was well arranged and supplied.

In the year after our Lord's birth 1605 on January 2nd four English ships also arrived in Bantam; they had lost most of their people on the voyage. The last name of that admiral was Middelton.[41]

On January 17th in the morning the ships sailed away out of Bantam with the intention of going to the Moluccas.

THE EIGHTH CHAPTER

About Cananor, Calicout, Cochyn and the Maldive Islands.[42]

Since mention was made in the last chapter of Cananor and some other cities and islands, it will be necessary to say something briefly about them before going any further with the description of the Sea Voyage already in hand.

First it should be known that the Portuguese hold and occupy some fine fortresses and cities in the whole region of Cabo de Ramos which lies 10 miles from Goa to the south (or midday) up to Cape Comoryn, formerly called Cory, Malabar. The first one

40. This information was brought by the ship *Medemblik*. It had sailed around Madagascar with the *Court of Holland*, but when the *Court* returned to Holland, *Medemblik* sailed to Bantam, arriving at the end of August. On December 31st it was reunited with the fleet.

41. For more on Sir Henry Middleton see the introduction.

42. This chapter has once again been adapted from Linschoten, *Itinerario*, vol. 1, chapters 11 and 13.

[fortress] is Onor [Honavar], the second is Barselor [near Coondapoor], the third is Mangalor, but the fourth and best is Cananor whose king told the Dutch that he wanted to maintain friendship with them since they did no damage to his fortress and Maldive Islands. The said city and fortress lie 11½ degrees from the equator, about 49 miles from Goa, and have much pepper growing around them. The Malabars, that is those native to the coast of Malabar, hold markets every day outside of the fortress in the city in which all kinds of food, like chickens, eggs, butter, honey, Indian oil, and figs (which are called Cananor's figs; the best and most beautiful are from India) are brought in such plenty that the markets are comparable to the weekly markets in Holland. Such beautiful and long wood for masts are brought there to sell — indeed no better ones are found in Norway — and in such quantities that all the surrounding regions are supplied with them. It is a very beautiful place, full of trees and very fruitful, as the whole area of Malabar is also.

Cananor is eleven miles from Calicout.[43] It lies at 11 degrees and somewhat more. Formerly this was the finest city on all of the Malabar Coast in the East Indies, where the Samoryn or Emperor lived. But because the Portuguese were often deceived by him when they first arrived in the Indies, they allied themselves with the King of Cochyn who was then the Samoryn's vassal. And then it happened that as [the number of] the Portuguese increased in that place and [they] became the most powerful on the water, Calicout became poorer and fell into decline; Cochyn and its king, however, rose so that now he is much richer and more powerful than the Samoryn.

43. Linschoten, *Itinerario*, vol. 1, p. 53, gives 8 miles.

Cochyn is 20 miles from Calicout. This city [Cochyn] is not much smaller than Goa, has very beautiful buildings, churches and cloisters, and also a very beautiful river on which ships can very easily sail. A little stream, which is sometimes very dry, runs not far from the city on the land side; next to it is a field called Cochyndayma, that is, over Cochyn, which belongs to the Malabar natives who still live in their superstition. That is where the king lives and also where he holds a market, which by far surpasses the other one. The Island of Cochyn has many little streams, which flow here and there, and also a large amount of pepper, in fact so much that each year two ships could easily be filled with it.

Concerning the islands of Maldiva or Malediva [the Maldives], they lie 60 miles to the west of Cape Comoryn; it is said that there are about 11,000 of them. Part of them are inhabited, the others are not, for the land is very low there, almost like in Cochyn. Some of the islands are dangerously covered with water, so that they cannot be seen. The people of Malabar like to say with truth that the islands were once connected to the main land of Malabar but in time were torn away from it by the sea (since they are so low lying.) There are no special wares to be found in these islands, except for Cocos or Indian nuts and Cayro the outer shell of those nuts which is hemp; all the ropes for Indian ships and other things are twisted from hemp. These nuts are found there in great numbers so that the inhabitants supply all of India. The ships of those inhabitants are made of coconut trees, the sails of the leaves and the ropes of the said coconut shells. Thus, their ships are built of nothing which does not come from the coconut trees, and even the food which they carry along comes from the same trees, so that this one tree sustains the inhabitants of the Maldive Islands. See the following diagram of Cape Comoryn and the surrounding places.

THE NINTH CHAPTER

*How the Dutch traveled from Bantam to the Molucca islands,
what they encountered on the way, and finally
how they captured Amboyna.*

At the end of the seventh chapter it was related how the Dutch ships in the year 1604 after the birth of our dear savior Jesus Christ safely arrived in Bantam in Java Major early in the morning on the 31st day of the month of December and on the 17th of the following January 1605 sailed again from there to the Moluccas. But before they went on such a voyage, they sailed to the Sunda Strait, where they took on fresh water and some firewood. Then to Iacadra [Jakarta] where they bought some provisions since they were very expensive in Bantam.

On the 28th of the former month [January] the yacht *Mozambique* and the sloops from the admiral's and vice-admiral's ships were loaded with some wares from the other ships, as well as some from the factor, and then left to go to Griessen [Gresik on Java]. Chief merchant [Hendrick Jacobsz.] Compostel travelled with them in order to observe whether there was something to trade in that place.[44]

44. According to Craen's diary, the yachts *Medemblik* and *Mozambique* were sent to Jakarta on January 10, followed by the rest of the fleet on January 22. He gives the departure date for the Moluccas as January 25. The yachts and sloops apparently traded along the coast of Java until met by the fleet at Gresik on January 28. ("Dagboek gehouden door H. J. Craen," pp. 181–183.) At the beginning of the seventeenth century Gresik (or Grise) belonged to the small kingdom of Surabaya and served as the chief port and mar-

On February 15th they recovered some loot from the Portuguese not far from Byma[45] when they overtook a ship in which they found the governor of the Moluccas along with many boxes of powder and ammunition. He came from Malacca and was traveling from there to Amboyna.

On the 21st towards evening they arrived in the bay or approach to Amboyna and anchored for the night on the north side.

The next day very early they exerted all possible effort to come close to the Portuguese fortress. But before they could reach it, a little boat was sent to them with two Portuguese from the captain, who brought and handed over a letter to the admiral. The content was as follows: the said captain desired to know what he [the admiral] was doing there with his ships? He had been commanded by His Majesty the King [of Portugal] to keep the fortress and therefore they ought to go quietly away from it. The admiral's answer to this was that although the governor was commanded by His Majesty to protect the fortress, so he, on the other hand, [was commanded] by his Excellency, Prince Maurice of Nassau[46] to come here to capture it as well as the whole island of Amboyna.

ket. It was not surprising that the Dutch fleet stopped at Gresik since it was not only a center for the spice trade but also a food exporting port. M. A. P. Meilink-Roelofsz, *Asian Trade and European Influence in the Indonesian Archipelago between 1550 and about 1630* (The Hague: Martinus Nijhoff, 1962), 269–71.

45. Bima was a port on the northern coast of Sumbawa. The Dutch, however, sometimes used the name Bima for the whole island. (Meilink-Roelofsz, *Asian Trade*, p. 353.) Craen states that the fleet remained at Bima for four days. ("Dagboek gehouden door H. J. Craen," p. 183.)

46. Count Maurice of Nassau (1566–1625) was the second son of William of Orange, leader of the Dutch revolt. Maurice did not inherit the title of Prince of Orange until the death of his older brother in 1618. The author has noted his correct title earlier.

The two Portuguese were very troubled by the admiral's answer, and therefore they soon took their leave with the firm assurance that they would bring a further reply from their commander. Meanwhile the ships did not stop exerting the greatest effort to come ever nearer the fortress, so that by the tenth hour of the morning they had arrived under it and had thrown out their anchor there.

When those in the fortress saw this, they came to the conclusion that it would be very difficult for them in the long run to hold out against the ships. So they sent out a merchant — before they suffered in the least — to speak with the ships. Finally after much discussion the following treaty was decided and resolved.

First, that all unmarried Portuguese should move elsewhere from the island; all married people who wanted could remain there if they swore faith and loyalty to the noble States General of the United Netherlands.

Secondly, that all who wished to leave could take a handgun with them. The ordnance, however, gunpowder, shot and other weapons belonging to the King were to be left undamaged in the fortress.

[Having concluded] this treaty the admiral with fifty men entered the fortress, placed the flag on the wall and let it fly. When those in the ships saw it, they fired off and shot all their guns in triumph.

This fortress was well supplied with thirty guns and all kinds of necessities. It was estimated that those who left the fortress and island numbered about 600 altogether. They were sent away in two ships which the Dutch had captured earlier.[47]

47. Craen identifies them as the yacht *Mozambique* and the ship captured near Bima; they sailed on March 13. ("Dagboek gehouden door H. J. Craen," p. 187.)

Forty-six Portuguese households remained there, and all committed themselves by oath to promote the best for and avoid harming the noble States General and his Excellency Prince Maurice of Nassau.

Although this victory was achieved easily—without effort or work—it should not therefore be esteemed less highly, for the place is of great importance and would not have been quickly captured if God had not given such a victory against all hope and expectation. And it could well be that God had wanted particularly to punish the Portuguese for the cruel massacre which they committed on this island in the year 1602.[48]

The Dutch resupplied the fortress with provisions for a whole year and appointed the chief merchant Friederich Holtzmann as governor of it.

Concerning Amboyna and its surroundings the reader should refer to the Second Sea Voyage in the 15th and 16th chapters.

THE TENTH CHAPTER

How the Dutch ships sailed to Tidore and there overwhelmed and burned two Portuguese carracks.

After Amboyna was captured in the manner described above, the Portuguese gone from it and everything within well disposed, the Dutch decided that five ships—namely the vice-admiral [*Dordrecht*], *Westfrießlandt*, *Amsterdam*, *Gelderland* and *Medenblick*—should go to Tidore, the admiral [*The United Provinces*] to Banda and the ship *Horen* should remain in Amboyna to take on its wares.

48. The massacre is referred to above in Chapter 1.

The island of Tidore is one of the finest in the Moluccas, on which so many cloves grow, that the whole world could be supplied.

It lies about 70 miles from Amboyna to the north (or midnight.) Six miles further on is the Island of Moluco and the next Ternate.[49] More information about these islands will be added in the next Relation; they have also been fully described by Levinius Hulsius of blessed memory in the Second Sea Voyage in the 31st and following chapters, to which we wish to refer the good reader for brevity's sake.

On May 5[50] the five ships which separated from the others at Amboyna came to the Island of Paulo Cauelii [now called Mare Island]; there they encountered the English Admiral Middelton who informed them that he had already filled part [of his ship with] cloves in Tidore and intended to go to Mackian to receive his full cargo.[51]

49. The author has again based his description on Linschoten (vol. 1, Chapter 21) whose information in this case is deficient. The five main Moluccan islands are Makian, Moti, Mare, Tidore and Ternate. Tidore and Ternate are less than five kilometers apart, and the small island between them is called Maitara.

50. This must be a typographical error. The chronology does not make sense unless it reads May 1, as given in de Bry's account. Johan Theodor and Johan Israel de Bry, Appendix to *Achter Theil der Orientalischen Indien* (Frankfurt, 1606), p. 23.

51. See the introduction for details of Middleton's voyage and the suspicions of the Dutch that he collaborated with the Portuguese during the siege of Tidore. The capture of Amboina had thwarted his hopes of purchasing cloves there, and so Middleton had hurried to reach the Moluccas before the Dutch. Although he arrived five weeks before Vice-admiral Bastiaensz. and reached an agreement with the Portuguese at Tidore, apparently selling gunpowder and provisions in exchange for cloves, he had only obtained a partial cargo and was on his way to Makian for more when he encountered the Dutch fleet. (Leonard Y. Andaya, *The World of Maluku: Eastern Indonesia in the Early Modern Period* [Honolulu: University of Hawaii Press, 1993], 139.)

When the ships asked him whether the fortress of Tidore was well supplied with boxes of gunpowder, he answered that they had a full 16 large tuns, which could not be true seeing that the governor of the Moluccas, who was captured near Byma (as already related), declared that those in Tidore had none or very little powder. Indeed the reason for his voyage to Malacca was to fetch gunpowder and other necessities for Amboyna and Tidore.

The English admiral also said (in what kind of spirit can easily be detected) that the Portuguese were resolved to test their strength against us and that the King of Tidore had firmly promised and sworn to assist the Portuguese against us.

On the second day of May the ships arrived at Tidore and anchored immediately across from the king's court in order to speak with him.

While they lay at anchor in this place they became aware of two carracks which were there to be loaded; guns had been placed on land on either side of the carracks so that they could very easily be protected.

On May 5th the vice-admiral demanded [the surrender] of the fortress of Tidore. The answer was that they refused his request and were determined to hold it down to the last man. With that answer it was soon decided and found good first to fire on the two carracks and take them from the Portuguese by force. Therefore the vice-admiral and the ship *Gelderland* attacked them. Jan Jansz. Mol who served as shipmaster [on the *Gelderland*], showed such courage that he is worthy of the highest fame. These two ships had the advantage and began immediately to thunder mightily at the carracks. The Portuguese on the other hand did not neglect to answer with the guns they had on land while the carracks [themselves] also answered bravely with guns and muskets; the balls fell so thick on each side as though there was a hail of musket and other balls.

One of the Dutch trumpeters who stood above on the ship blowing the trumpet was shot along with others, and he fell down into the ship.

During this shooting the vice-admiral and Jan Jansz. Mol filled their two boats or yachts with men and rowed them to the carracks, boarded them and after enduring an hour-long fight, actually captured and took them. Most of the people who were on board sprang into the water, for they had laid a match next to the boxes of gunpowder in order to blow up the carrack which they could no longer hold. But the Dutch became aware of it as soon as they arrived. In this conflict three of their people were left dead, and 17 wounded. What was found in the carracks was [not] worth [much], so after they removed twelve guns — both large and small — they set the ships on fire and let them drift away.[52]

The Eleventh Chapter

The Siege and Capture of the Fortress at Tidore.

Although the Portuguese lost their two carracks and could not accomplish anything with their heavy bombardment, nevertheless they did not lose courage but persisted in their determination to hold the fortress to the end. When the Dutch realized this, they considered the matter and conferred with the King of Ternate who thought it advisable to wait a few days before attacking the fortress until he could gather his forces so that the

52. Craen, whose ship *Gelderland* took part in the capture, writes that both ships were empty, waiting to be loaded. The carracks burned for two days. ("Dagboek gehouden door H. J. Craen," pp. 189–90.)

capture would be the easier. The reason for this request was that he well knew (so he said) that the Portuguese were well supplied by the English with gunpowder, shot, bread, wine, fish and other necessities.

Now since the King of Ternate's forces had been brought to another's land, it was thought advisable to seek to negotiate with the King of Tidore in order to prevent a great spilling of blood. If he were willing to let the Dutch deal with the Portuguese alone without his assistance, the King of Ternate would in return also remain quiet and not help the Dutch. The King of Tidore was finally content with this condition. After making this treaty between the Kings of Tidore and Ternate, 150 men from the five ships went on land to attack the fortress by force. They were led by the shipmaster Mol; the captain of the Zeeland ship named de la Parte was assigned to him as an assistant, and during this capture he showed himself to be a brave soldier.[53] When they landed they went first to two Portuguese villages which lay one to the south (or midday) and one to the north and set fire to them in order to frighten those in the fortress.

Meanwhile the King of Ternate who had [a total of] fourteen Caracolles[54] each with 140 men, came on land with 500 of his men in order to show what the outcome of the present fight

53. It is not clear if this was the ship *Seelandt* or another ship. The skipper of the *Zeeland* is given as Quirin Pieter above; perhaps "de la Parte" (later also de la Perre) was the unidentified captain of the soldiers. The *Nieuw Nederlandsch Biografisch Woordenboek* lists several members of the van de Perre family as merchants and citizens of Middelburg (in Zeeland) at the end of the sixteenth century, but I have been unable to identify this man more closely.

54. A "kora-kora" was a Moluccan boat with double outriggers. Andaya (p. 283) notes that ordinary ones had a crew of 50–70 men but the largest could hold 200. These vessels are clearly depicted on the engraving of the siege of Tidore.

would be and especially to deter the King of Tidore by means of his presence from giving any help or aid to the Portuguese.

After the departure of their men, the five Dutch ships moved to the north side of the fortress, and from there they began to shoot fiercely. Captain Mol thereby received the opportunity to come nearer the fortress.

He quickly erected two batteries from wine casks filled with earth which were worked on day and night; then the fortress was also fired upon hard from [the batteries.] The Portuguese, for their part, were not behind in bombarding. Now because seamen are not nearly so skilled at lying low for a long time, Captain Mol with two soldiers [soon] moved closer to the fortress in order to inspect it. When he found that the guns had made a breach which could easily be stormed, it was decided that they should try to storm it on the following day. When day came — which was May 19th — the shipmaster Mol brought all his men stealthily and in such a way to the fortress that those in it were not aware. Those in the ships continued bravely with the bombardment until Captain Mol, having completed his march, flew a small flag on the embankment as a sign that they should stop. Those in the ships immediately remained quiet and Mol with his men attacked the fortress from both sides. After a long fight he and eight others entered with a small flag. But the Portuguese prevented any more from entering by hard gunfire and especially by fire pots which they threw in great numbers from the fortress towers (the small flag was burned in this way.) When those in the fortress realized [what had happened] they took courage and drove Mol and the other seven who had remained in the fortress for a quarter of an hour out again. During the retreat Mol fell from the wall and broke his leg. Some of his soldiers would gladly have helped him get away, but he would not allow it. Instead he shouted that they should attack [the fortress] a second time. He did this for so long until finally someone came who took him on his shoulders and carried him away from there. In this first attack a Portuguese captain from one of the captured carracks who had escaped to the fortress was killed. He was the first one to come against Captain Mol meaning to stab him with his rapier or spear but the Captain deflected the thrust with a small spear which he had in his hand;[55] he broke it when he stabbed the Portuguese who was in full armour. After that the Captain knocked him down, and they struggled so long together until a musket shot intervened. The Portuguese captain was shot through the head and fell to the ground.

Having repelled this first storming the Portuguese turned back the second one more easily than the first since those in the fortress were much more courageous than before; they even came out of the fortress and pursued our men half way to their fortification. When the ships noticed it, they began again to fire bravely on the fortress. During the bombardment, however, it happened that the ship *Gelderland* shot at the great tower and the ball fell into the fortress; the tower with 60 or 70 men on it exploded into the air with a terrible noise (as can easily be imagined). Then the Dutch seamen and soldiers attacked for the third time and took and captured the fortress. The rest of the Portuguese cried as best they could for mercy which was also granted to them.

55. The author uses the terms "pertuisanen oder Knebelspieß" and "Spießlein" for the weapons in this fight. De Bry gives the Portuguese captain a "rapier" and Mol a "Knebelspieß." (Appendix to *Achter Theil der Orientalischen Indien*, p. 25.)

Until then those from Ternate had remained quiet, but when they saw that the fortress was taken, they also ran up to it and plundered it heavily, destroying and ruining everything.

In the fortress there was a stone tower full of cloves which was set on fire and ruined in spite of the fact that the Dutch did their best to turn them [the Ternatans] away and preserve the tower.

On the Dutch side no more than two were killed in the capture and seven wounded, including Captain Mol whose leg was broken.

On the Portuguese side seventy-three were killed and twelve or thirteen wounded. Their women, for the most part, had saved themselves in a fort situated on a great height; it could only be reached by an extremely narrow path so that this fortress could not be captured except through starvation or lack of water.

Some sloops or boats were given to the captured Portuguese and their women and children, in which they — about 500 of them young and old altogether — sailed away to the Philippines, also called Lussones and Manillas.

It is still unknown how the fire reached the boxes of gunpowder in the fortress, whether it occurred through the ships' bombardment or the carelessness of the Portuguese. It is certain, however, that if it had not happened, it would have been very difficult for the Dutch to capture the fortress with so few men.

On the approval of the council the fortress was fully razed since it was already ruined and blown up.

*Key for the most important things which are marked
on the following map of the island and fortress of Tidore.*

A. Mesquite, that is the temple of the inhabitants.

B. A village in the south of the island which was burned by the Dutch.

C. Two batteries or places for guns made by the Portuguese to protect the two carracks.

D. The two carracks which the Dutch overwhelmed and captured.

E. The city of the Moors.

F. Their church.

G. The king's court.

H. The city where the Portuguese lived.

I. The Portuguese prayerhouse.

K. The fortress of Tidore.

L. The boats which brought the Dutch to the land to storm the fortress.

M. Caracolles of the King of Ternate.

N. A village on the north side of the island of Tidore which the Dutch set fire to in order to frighten those in the fortress.

O. The King of Ternate, the friend of the Dutch.

P. Captain Jan Jansz. Mol who has the advantage.

Q. Captain de la Perre, from the *Seelandt*.

R. The place where the King of Ternate remained to watch the battle.

S. The batteries or places for guns made of wine casks on which the Dutch placed their guns to bombard the fortress.

pag. 49.

I. Des P. Frieslant

Amsterdam

T. A skirmish between the Dutch and Portuguese when they wanted to approach the fortress.

V. The storming of the fortress.

W. The great thick tower from which the Portuguese defended themselves with fire works and other things and which was finally blown up by gunpowder.

X. A fort on a very tall and high hill on which many cloves grew and into which the Portuguese women and children went.

Z. The ship of the English admiral [Middelton].

AA. The 2 Portuguese carracks which were burned by the Dutch.

THE TWELFTH CHAPTER

How the Dutch settled [affairs] in Tidore and how
two of the twelve outbound ships returned home.

The vice-admiral not only razed the captured fortress of Tidore in order to win the favor of the inhabitants who had been restrained by it but also particularly ordered some of his people, who were to remain there to trade with the inhabitants, to be mediators between the two kings of Ternate and Tidore. Thereafter the ship *Gelderland* sailed to Ternate where it took on a good load of cloves and arrived again in Bantam on July 24th.

On the 25th of the same month [July] it went with the ship *Tergoude* to return home, and, God be praised, they arrived safely in May of the past year 1606 bringing us the news of the capture of Amboyna and Tidore.[56] It is hoped that with God's help

---

56. The ship *Gouda* (150 *last*) was sent out in June 1604 after the rest of the fleet had sailed. According to Craen, it had joined the ships *Zeeland* and *Enchuysen* — and

the other ships will shortly return home, as well as those which sailed with Warwygk.[57]

When there is something special to report concerning these [ships], as is expected, it will be done; in particular, though, anything about Warwygk will be imparted to you, good reader, in the appendix of this Ninth or in the following Tenth Sea Voyage. Meanwhile, farewell. The end.

with them had defeated six Portuguese carracks — before meeting the *Gelderland* at Bantam in August, 1605. ("Dagboek gehouden door H. J. Craen," pp. 202–3.)

57. Wybrandt van Warwijck was the commander of the first expedition sent to the East Indies by the VOC in 1602. He did not return until 1607, and thus the outcome of this first voyage was not known when this pamphlet was published.

Appendix

The author of the Ninth Sea Voyage not only translated an account of Steven van der Haghen's voyage to the East Indies but also Germanized the names of the ships and the officers. The following table shows the differences in the names of the ships and the officers (as well as discrepancies in the size of the vessels) according to *The Ninth Sea Voyage* (1606)—line one; Isaak Commelin (1646)—line two; and de Jonge—line three.[1]

Names of the Ships and Officers

Ship	Schiffman or schipper	size (Last)	Opperkoopman
1. Die vereinigte Provinzen	Simon Hun°	350	
Vereenichde Provincien (A)	Simon Hoen	350	
Vereenigde Provintien	Simon Jansz. Hoen		Jan Willemsz. Verschoor
2. Dordrecht	Hans Reimelandt°	500	
Dordrecht (Z)	Hans Rymelandt	350	
Dordrecht	Hans Riemlandt		
3. Amsterdam	Arnold Clasen Calckbuys°	350	
Amsterdam (A)	Arent Claesz. Calck-huys	350	
Amsterdam	Arendt Claesz. Calckbuys		Frederik de Houtman°

1. Izaak Commelin, *Begin ende Voortgangh der Vereenighde Nederlantsche Geoctroyeerde Oost-indische Compagnie* (1646), 2:2–3. J. K. J. de Jonge, *De Opkomst van het Nederlandsche Gezag in Oost-Indie (1595–1610)* (1865), 3:27–28. Only de Jong lists the names of the merchants on board each ship which he found in the Rijks-Archief (though without supplying any specific bibliographic information.)

4. Westfrießlandt	Jacob Jacob Sohn Clunt°	250	
West-Vrieslandt (HE)	Iacob Iacobsz. Clunt	350	
Westfriesland	Jacob Jacobsz. Clunt		Robbert Outerman°
5. Groß Horen	Johan Cornelis Sohn°	350	
Hoorn (HE)	Ian Cornelisz. Avenhorn	350	
Hoorn	Jan Cornelisz. Avenhorn		Hendric Jacobsz. Compostel
6. Gelderland	Johan Johan Sohn Moll°	250	
Gelderlandt (A)	Ian Iansz. Mol	250	
Gelderland	Jan Jansz. Mol		Hendrick Janssen Craen
7. Seelandt	Quirin Pieter	250	
Zeelandia (Z)	Cryn Pietersz.	250	
Zeeland	Crijn Pietersz.		Abraham Awijn
8. Hoffe von Hollandt	Wilhelm Lock	180	
't Hof van Hollandt (A)	Willem Cornelisz Schout	180	
Hof van Hollant	Willem Lock		Pieter Dirckz.
9. Delfft	Wilhelm Cornelis Sohn Schultheiß	150	
Delft (A)	Willem Lock	150	
Delft	Willem Cornelisz. Schouten		Guillam Lodewycx
			Paulus van Soldt
			Pieter Ysaäcx Eyloff
10. Enchuysen	Claes Theissen Caller	150	
Enckhuysen (HE)	Claes Thijsz. Cul	150	
Enkhuizen	Claes Tijssen Caller		
11. Medenblik	Dierick Claes Sohn	126	
Medenblick (HE)	Dirrick Claesz Moylieves	125	
Medemblik	Dirck Claessen MoyLievens		Cornelis Segertsz.
12. Täublein	Johann Wilhelm Sohn+	36	
Het Duysken (A)	Willem Iansz.	30	
Duyfke	Willem Jansz of Jansen		

A = outfitted by the Amsterdam chamber
Z = outfitted by the Zeeland chamber
HE = outfitted by the Hoorn and Enkhuizen chambers

° = member of the Council of War

+ De Jonge notes (p. 42) that there was some confusion between the skipper of the ship *Little Dove*, Willem Jansz. and the president of the Dutch factory at Bantam, Jan Willemsz.

Most of these ships had seen previous service to the East Indies.[2] *Dordrecht* sailed in 1600; *Amsterdam* in 1595, 1598 and 1600; *Hoorn* in 1601; *Gelderland* in 1601; *Zeeland*[3] in 1601; *Hof van Hollant* in 1599; *Delft* in 1600; *Enkhuizen* in 1601 and *Duyfke* in 1595 and 1601. A ship by the name of *Vereenigde Landen* sailed east in 1599, although it is not clear if it was the same as the *Vereenigde Provintien*. Likewise the *Vriesland* mentioned as part of a fleet of ten ships in 1599 might have been the same as the *Westfriesland*.[4] Only the name *Medemblik* does not appear in any of the previous voyages described by de Jonge.

The captains and merchants are harder to indentify, but some certainly had previously sailed to Asia. Vice-admiral Cornelis Bastiaensz. had been part of a Middelburg fleet in 1601 as captain of the *Zeelandia*. Simon Jansz. Hoen had participated on van Neck's two expeditions of 1598 and 1600 as the skipper of two smaller ships (one was the *Delft*.) There was a merchant Jacob Jacobsz. on the *Delft* in 1600, although he is not given the surname Clunt. Jan Cornelisz. served as the skipper of the *Zeeland* and Willem Cornelisz. Schouten as skipper of the *Duyfke* with Hermansz.'s fleet of 1601. Willem Jansz., the discoverer of Australia, was the first mate (opperstuurman) on board the *Hollandia* in 1599.

2. I have assumed that the name is an adequate indentification of the vessel. Thus the ship *Amsterdam* which sailed with the first Dutch voyage to the East Indies in 1595 is the same as the *Amsterdam* which sailed with the second fleet in 1598. This need not be so, but the chronology works every time except for the case of *Zeeland/Zeelandia* as noted below. De Jonge, vol. 2, contains extensive lists of the ships and crew for the voyages before 1603.

3. The *Zeelandia* sailed with van Neck in 1598 and with a Middelburg fleet in 1601. It was evidently a different ship from the *Zeeland*, however, since it could not have sailed with both the Middelburg and Amsterdam fleets in 1601. Commelin uses the name *Zeelandia*.

4. A yacht named *Vriesland* which sailed with van Neck in 1598 was clearly not the same as the *Westfriesland* since it was too large to be classed as a yacht. It is not clear whether the *Vriesland* mentioned in 1599 was the same yacht or not.

Bibliography

Primary Sources:

Bijdragen en Mededeelingen van het Historisch Genootschap Utrecht 6 (1883):

"Instructie ende Ordonnantie (voor van der Haghen)," pp. 258-65.

"Remonstrantie ende vertoch van van der Haghen," pp. 265-80.

"Cort verhael van 't geene bij den Admirael Steuen vander Haghen tot Ambonen met de Portugesen ende Jesuyten gehandelt is," pp. 281-92.

"Journaal van Steven van der Haghen," pp. 292-337.

"Accord van Steven van der Hagen met de Portugeezen te Ambon in d. 3 Mrt. 1605," pp. 337-38.

"Beschrijuinge vant eylant, stadt ende casteel van Ambona, enz.," pp. 338-76.

Commelin, Izaak. *Begin ende Voortgangh der Vereeinghde Nederlantsche Geoctroyeerde Oost-indische Compagnie. Begrijpende de volghende tvvaelf Voyagien, door de Inwoonderen der selviger Provintien derwaerts gedaen.* 1646.

De Bry, Johan Theodor and Johan Israel. *Achter Theil der Orientalischen Indien.* Frankfurt, 1606.

Jonge, J. K. J. de. *De Opkomst van het Nederlandsch Gezag in Oost-Indie (1595-1610).* Vol. 3. The Hague: Martinus Nijhoff, 1865:

"Instructie voor den admiraal Steven van der Hagen," pp. 146-63.

"Uittreksels uit het dagboek gehouden door Hendrick Jansz. Craen, aan boord van het schip Gelderland, gezeild op den 18 Dec. uit Texel," pp. 164-204.

"Contract tusschen den admiraal Steven van der Hagen en den Samoryn of Keyzer van Malabar op den 11n Novber 1604," pp. 204-5.

"Extract uit de ordonnantie en instructie voor de cooplieden, assistente, enz. de van wege de Generale Comp. tot Bantam zullen blyven, vastgesteld, Decber 1603, pp. 206-8.

"Accoort van Capitan, oock de Hoofden van Hitoe ende den admirael Steven van der Hagen. Febr. 1605," pp. 208-10.

"Contract gesloten tusschen den admiraal Steven van der Hagen en de overheden van de eilanden van Banda c.a.," pp. 210-13.

Linschoten, Jan Huygen van. *Itinerario. Voyage ofte Schipvaert van Jan Huyghen van Linschoten naer Oost ofte Portugaels Indien 1579-1592.* 2nd ed. 3 vols. H. Kern and H. Terpstra, eds. The Hague: Martinus Nijhoff, 1955-57.

The Voyage of Sir Henry Middleton to the Moluccas, 1604-06. William Foster, ed. London: Hakluyt Society, 1943.

SECONDARY SOURCES:

Akveld, L. M.; Bosscher, Ph. M.; Bruijn, J. R.; and Oosten, F. C. van. *Vier Eeuwen Varen: Kapiteins, Kapers, Kooplieden en Geleerden.* Bussum, 1973.

Andaya, Leonard Y. *The World of Maluku: Eastern Indonesia in the Early Modern Period.* Honolulu: University of Hawaii Press, 1993.

Baker, William A. *Sloops and Shallops.* Columbia, SC: University of South Carolina Press, 1966.

Boxer, C. R. *The Dutch Seaborne Empire 1600-1800.* London: Hutchinson, 1965; reprinted New York: Alfred Knopf, 1970.

_____. *The Portuguese Seaborne Empire 1415-1825*. New York: Alfred Knopf, 1969.

Davies, D. W. *A Primer of Dutch Seventeenth Century Overseas Trade*. The Hague: Martinus Nijhoff, 1961.

De Vries, Jan. *The Dutch Rural Economy in the Golden Age, 1500-1700*. New Haven: Yale University Press, 1974.

Israel, Jonathan I. *Dutch Primacy in World Trade, 1585-1740*. Oxford: Clarendon Press, 1989.

Jonge, J. K. J. de. *De Opkomst van het Nederlandsch Gezag in Oost-Indie*. 13 vols. The Hague: Martinus Nijhoff, 1862-88.

Kemp, Peter, ed. *The Oxford Companion to Ships and the Sea*. London: Oxford University Press, 1976.

Keuning, J. "Ambonese, Portuguese and Dutchmen: The History of Ambon to the End to the Seventeenth Century," in Meilink-Roelofsz, M. A. P. et al., *Dutch Authors on Asian History: A Selection of Dutch Historiography on the Verenigde Oostindische Compagnie*. Dordrecht: Foris Publications, 1988, pp. 362-97.

Landwehr, John. *VOC: A Bibliography of Publications Relating to the Dutch East India Company, 1602-1800*. Utrecht: Hes Publishers, 1991.

Masselman, George. *The Cradle of Colonialism*. New Haven: Yale University Press, 1963.

Meilink-Roelofsz, M. A. P. *Asian Trade and European Influence in the Indonesian Archipelago between 1500 and about 1630*. The Hague: Martinus Nijhoff, 1962.

_____. "Steven van der Haghen," in Akveld, L. M. et al. *Vier Eeuwen Varen: Kapiteins, Kapers, Kooplieden en Geleerden*. Bussum, 1973, pp. 26-49.

Meilink-Roelofsz, M. A. P.; van Opstall, M. E.; and Schutte, G. J., eds. *Dutch Authors on Asian History: A Selection of Dutch Historiography on the Verenigde Oostindische Compagnie*. Dordrecht: Foris Publications, 1988.

Bibliography

Parry, J.H. *The Establishment of the European Hegemony, 1415-1715: Trade and Exploration in the Age of the Renaissance.* 3rd rev. ed. New York: Harpertorchbook, 1966.

Phillips, Carla Rahn. "The growth and composition of trade in the Iberian empires, 1450-1750," in James D. Tracy, ed. *The Rise of Merchant Empires: Long-Distance Trade in the Early Modern World, 1350-1750.* Cambridge: Cambridge University Press, 1990, pp. 34-101.

Roelofsz, M. Antoinette P. *De Vestiging der Nederlanders ter Kuste Malabar.* Verhandelingen van het Koninklijk Instituut voor de Taal-, Land- en Volkenkunde van Nederlandsch-Indie, Deel 4. The Hague: Martinus Nijhoff, 1943.

Royen, P. C. van. *Zeevardenden op de Koopvaardijvloot Omstreeks 1700.* Hollandse Historische Reeks, no. VIII. Amsterdam: De Bataafsche Leeuw, 1987.

Smith, Alan K. *Creating a World Economy: Merchant Capital, Colonialism, and World Trade, 1400-1825.* Boulder: Westview Press, 1991.

Steensgaard, Niels. *The Asian Trade Revolution of the Seventeenth Century: The East India Companies and the Decline of the Caravan Trade.* Chicago: University of Chicago Press, 1973.

_____. *Carracks, Caravans and Companies: The Structural Crisis in the European-Asian Trade in the Early Seventeenth Century.* Scandinavian Institute of Asian Studies, no. 17. Denmark: Andelsbogtrykkeriet i Odense, 1973.

_____. "The growth and composition of the long-distance trade of England and the Dutch Republic before 1750," in James D. Tracy, ed. *The Rise of Merchant Empires: Long-Distance Trade in the Early Modern World, 1350-1750.* Cambridge: Cambridge University Press, 1990, pp. 102-152.

Subrahmanyam, Sunjay. *The Portuguese Empire in Asia, 1500-1700: A Political and Economic History.* London: Longman, 1993.

Bibliography

Tiele, P. A. *Mémoire Bibliographique sur les Journaux des Navigateurs Néerlandais*. Amsterdam: Frederik Muller, 1867.

_____. "Steven van der Haghen's avonturen van 1575 tot 1597." *Bijdraden en Mededeelingen van het Historisch Genootschap Utrecht 6* (1883): 377-421.

Tracy, James D. *True Ocean Found: Paludanus's Letters on Dutch Voyages to the Kara Sea, 1595-1596*. Minneapolis: University of Minnesota Press, 1980.

_____. *Holland Under Habsburg Rule, 1506-1566: The Formation of a Body Politic*. Berkeley: University of California Press, 1990.

_____, ed. *The Rise of Merchant Empires: Long-Distance Trade in the Early Modern World, 1350-1750*. Cambridge: Cambridge University Press, 1990.

_____. "Herring wars: The Habsburg Netherlands and the Struggle for Control of the North Sea, ca. 1520-1560." *Sixteenth Century Journal* 24 (1993): 249-272.

Unger, Richard. *Dutch Shipbuilding before 1800: Ships and Guilds*. Assen and Amsterdam: Van Gorcum, 1978.

Wittmann, Reinhard. *Geschichte des deutschen Buchhandels: Ein Überblick*. Munich: C. H. Beck, 1991.

Index

Achin (Achyn), 25, 78
Africa, 8, 12, 21, 22, 40
Alkmaer (Alkmaar) (ship), 51, 78
ambergris (gray amber), 63
Amboina (Amboyna), 11, 30, 31, 32,
    38, 82; alliance with van der
    Haghen (1600), 18, 26; arrival of
    the Dutch fleet at, 83; massacre
    at (1602), 16, 46, 87; people of,
    26-27, 46; surrender of, 83-87;
    under Dutch control, 17, 27-28;
    under Portuguese control, 26
ammunition, 9, 75, 83, 86, 91
Amsterdam, 8, 10, 20, 49, 52; trad-
    ing companies of, 9, 18, 41n, 51n
Amsterdam (ship), 20, 50, 74n, 76n,
    87, 100, 102
Antogil, Bay of, 51, 78
Antwerp, 4, 9, 18
Arabia: merchants of, 65
Armenia: merchants of, 65
Australia, 33, 102
Awijn, Abraham, 101

Banda Islands, 17, 31, 32, 51, 87
Bantam, 25, 33, 50, 79; arrival of
    the Dutch fleet at, 52, 78, 82, 98;

arrival of the English fleet at, 30,
    31, 79; Portuguese attack on, 45-
    46
Bardes, 68, 69, 70, 71, 72
Barselor, 80
Bastiaensz. (or Sebastiansz.), Cor-
    nelis (vice-admiral), 20n, 49-50,
    78n, 102; at the siege of Tidore,
    31, 32, 87, 89, 90; negotiations
    with the King of Calicut, 74, 75
Batavia, 23
Bayxos dos India (shoals of India),
    58
Bengala: merchants of, 65
Bima (Byma), 83, 89
Brabant, 3, 4
Brazil, 40
bread, 91
butter, 80

Cabo de Ramos, 79
Calckbuys, Arnold Clasen (Arent
    Claesz.), 21n, 50, 100
Calicut (Calicout), 24, 65, 73, 75,
    79, 81; arrival of the Dutch fleet
    at, 74-77; description of, 80
Calicut, King (or Samorin) of, 24,

108

monsoons, 22

Moors, 57, 61, 70, 71, 73, 74, 95

Moylieves, Dirrick, Claesz. *See* Claesz., Dierick

Mozambique, 21, 52, 65; description of, 57-63; Dutch hostilities against, 22, 54-56; governor of, 62; people of, 56-57, 60-61, 63; Portuguese fortress of, 54, 60

Mozambique (captured yacht), 22, 56, 57n, 82, 86n; rejoined the fleet, 76

muskets, 90, 93

Natal (Terra do Notallo), 58

naval skirmishes: at Cannanore, 24, 74-76; at Goa 24, 64-65

Neck, Jacob van, 9, 41, 51n, 102

Netherlands, 3, 4, 7, 9

New Guinea, 33

Niger River, 62

northeast passage, 39

Norway, 80

Nuremberg, 14

nutmeg, 11, 30, 31, 32

oil, 72, 80

Onor (Honavar), 80

Ontermann (Outerman), Robbert, 20n, 76, 101

Ormuz, 23

pangaye (or pangaios) (boat), 56, 62

Paulo Cauelii, Island of (Mare Island), 88

Pegu: merchants of, 65

pepper, 52, 78n, 80, 81

Persia: merchants of, 65

pewter, 52

Philip II, King of Spain and Portu-

gal, 7, 9n, 47

Philippines, 39, 94

Pieter, Quirin (Crijn), 50, 91n, 101

pork, 60

Portugal, 10, 29, 35, 38, 55, 69, 71

Portugal, King of, 7, 65, 69, 83, 86

Portuguese treatment of Dutch merchants, 17, 38, 40, 41, 44, 45, 46, 47

Portuguese empire, 4, 7, 23

radicem China, 52

Red Sea, 61

Reimelandt (Rijmelant), Hans, 20n, 50, 100

Reynst, Gerard, 19

rice, 56, 59, 72

S. Cathalina (*S. Catharina*) (ship), 51

S. George, Island of, 59, 60

S. Jacob, Island of, 59, 60

S. Thomas, Island of, 61

Salsette, Island of, 68, 69, 70, 72

Samorin (Samoryn). *See* Calicut, King of

Sao Tiago, Island of, 52, 54

Schouten (Schultheiß), Willem (Wilhelm) Cornelisz., 50, 101, 102

Sebastiansz., Cornelis. *See* Bastaiensz., Cornelis

Segertsz., Cornelis, 101

Sena, 61

sheep, 60

shipbuilding, 4, 5, 8

ships, types of: carrack, 21, 22, 34, 51, 54, 55, 56, 63, 69, 76, 87, 89, 90, 93, 95, 98; frigate, 24, 64, 65,

74, 75; fust, 45; galleon, 45; galley, 39, 45, 64; herringbus, 5; junk, 75; sloop, 54, 65, 74, 75, 94; yacht, 22, 33, 56n, 90

shot. *See* ammunition

Siam (Sian): merchants of, 65

silk, 4, 51

slaves, 63

Sofala (Soffala), 61, 62

Soldt, Paulus van, 101

Spain, 7, 9, 10, 18, 29, 30, 34, 38, 39

Spain, King of, 7, 39, 47, 62. *See also* Philip II

States General, 39, 47, 48, 87; instructions for fleets to the East Indies, 16, 21

States of Holland, 9

storms, 52

sugar, 52

Sumatra, Island of, 52n, 78

Sunda Strait, 82

Tartary, 39

Tergoude (*Gouda*) (ship), 98

Ternate, 11, 30, 44, 87, 88; rivalry with Tidore, 28-29

Ternate, King (or Sultan) of, 26, 29, 90, 91, 94, 95, 98

Texel, 18, 25, 33, 50, 52

Thyssen, Nickels, 76

Tidore, 11, 15, 16, 31, 32, 38, 44, 87, 88, 89; captured by the Dutch, 25, 28, 29-30, 31, 32, 98; fortress of, 29, 89, 90, 92, 93, 94, 95; rivalry with Ternate, 28-29; siege of, 55, 89-94

Tidore, King of, 29-30, 89, 91, 92, 98

Tournai, 18

travel literature, 11-12

trees, 69, 70, 80; banana (Indian fig), 59; bitter orange, 59; lemon, 59, nut, 59; palm, 59, 68, 69

United East India Company. *See* Verenigde Oost-Indische Compagnie (VOC)

United Provinces (*Vereenigde Provintien*) (ship), 20, 32, 49, 87, 100, 102

Verenigde Oost-Indische Compagnie (VOC), 11, 21, 48; chambers of, 10, 19-20, 49, 52, 100-101; formation of, 10, 16, 48-49; second voyage of, 18, 34, 48, 49, 50, 52

Verschoor, Jan Willemsz., 100

Warwijk (Warwygk), Wybrandt van, 99

weapons, 60, 86; firepots, 92; rapier, 93; spear, 93

West Indies, 40

Westfriesland (*Westfrießlandt*) (ship), 20, 50, 76n, 87, 101, 102

Wilhelmsz., Johann, 50, 101, 102

wine, 72, 91

Ypres, 18

Zeeland, 5, 10, 19, 20, 37n, 47, 48, 49, 52

Zeeland (*Seelandt*) (ship), 20, 50, 91, 95, 98n, 101, 102; sailed to Cambaya, 24, 77

113

Donors

Andersen, Elmer and Eleanor
Anderson, Carlyle E. and
  Elizabeth W.
Anderson, LaJean
Anonymous
Aris, Rutherford and Claire
Bell, Charles H.
Bell, Dr. and Mrs. Ford W.
Bell, Samuel H., Jr.
Dahlquist, Sally
Doerr, Wallace F.
Fredrickson, Arnold G.
Frye, John
General Mills Foundation
Hasselquist, Lorraine S.
Hattendorf, John B.
Heegaard, Lucy Hartwell
James Ford Bell Book Trust
Johnson, Carol A.
Jones, Ruth E.
Kellogg, Martin and Esther
Kittleson, J. Harold
Kreidberg, Irving and Marjorie
Laird, Mr. and Mrs. William P.
Lester, Dr. and Mrs. Richard G.

Martayan Lan, Inc.
Martin, Dr. Wilfred Finny
McCarthy, Mr. and Mrs. Donald W.
Mott, Gordon B.
Muck, Thomas and Bernadette
Myren, Frederick
Neimann, Diane B.
O'Connell, Thomas F.
Parker, John
Pesat, Adolphe A., III
Quinn, David
Reister, Ruth and Ray
Richardson, Jessie F.
Roy, Mr. and Mrs. Curtis L.
Rubin, Robert H., (Books)
Russell-Wood, A.J.R.
Savage, Elizabeth Z.
Schweitzer, Mary-Eliot
Simler, Lucy
Smith, Jean and Bill
Tiblin, Mariann
Tracy, James
Urness, Carol
Wulling, Emerson G.